College Reading Skills

Topics for the Restless, Book Two
Stimulating Selections for Indifferent Readers
Second Edition

Edward Spargo, Editor

Books in the Series:
Book One   Book Three
Book Two   Book Four

JAMESTOWN PUBLISHERS
a division of NTC/CONTEMPORARY PUBLISHING GROUP
Lincolnwood, Illinois USA

Topics for the Restless, Book Two

Second Edition

ISBN: 0-89061-528-4

Published by Jamestown Publishers,
a division of NTC/Contemporary Publishing Group, Inc.,
4255 West Touhy Avenue,
Lincolnwood (Chicago), Illinois 60646-1975 U.S.A.

8 9 0 VP 11 10 9 8 7 6 5 4

Cover credit: Copyright ARS N.Y./Succession
H. Matisse, 1989

Inside Front Cover: THE BETTMAN ARCHIVE, INC.
2 The Day I Nearly Drowned: AP/WIDE WORLD PHOTOS
3 Killer: Autobiography of a Mafia Hit Man: P. J. Heller
4 Aged Wait in Stony Solitude, but Not for Buses: Jeff Greenberg
5 Lost in Space: Alan Carey/The Image Works
6 Body Language Spoken Here: © by David Kreider/Photo Agora
7 The Pedestrian: UPI/BETTMANN NEWSPHOTOS
8 The Feminine Mystique: UPI/BETTMANN NEWSPHOTOS
9 Curbing Cab Crime in Chicago: Photo by Ben Merkel/Twilight Taxi Parts, Inc.
10 Virtuoso: Illustration by Julie Sardelli
11 First Flight Across America: Andrea Wade
12 The Standard of Living: UPI/BETTMANN NEWSPHOTOS
13 Letter from France: API/WIDE WORLD PHOTOS
14 Velcro: The Final Frontier: Photo courtesy of The National Broadcasting Company, Inc.
15 Marilyn: An Untold Story: UPI/BETTMANN NEWSPHOTOS
16 The Open Window: Illustration by Rich Bishop
17 Henry Ford's Fabulous Flivver: Ford Motor Company
18 Golden Oldies: Photo courtesy of The National Broadcasting Company, Inc.
19 When Pain is the Only Choice: American Cancer Society
20 Women in Prison: Copyright © Andy Levin, 1987. All Rights Reserved.

Readability			
Book One	F–G	Book Three	J–K
Book Two	H–I	Book Four	L–up

Acknowledgments

Acknowledgment is gratefully made to the following publishers and authors for permission to reprint these selections.

The Day I Nearly Drowned by June Mellies Reno. Copyright © 1974 by the Hearst Corporation. Reprinted by permission of *Good Housekeeping* magazine, the author, and Scott Meredith Literary Agency, Inc., 580 Fifth Avenue, New York, NY 10036.

Killer: Autobiography of a Mafia Hit Man. Reprinted with permission of Playboy Press from *Killer* by Joey with Dave Fisher. Copyright © 1973 by Playboy Press.

Aged Wait in Stony Solitude, but Not for Buses by McCandlish Phillips. From *The New York Times*, February 11, 1970. Copyright © 1970 by The New York Times Company and reprinted with their permission.

Lost in Space by Isaac Asimov. Reprinted by permission of the author.

Body Language Spoken Here by Elizabeth McGough. From *American Youth* magazine, August/September 1972. Reprinted by special permission of American Youth Magazine.

The Pedestrian. From *The Golden Apples of the Sun* by Ray Bradbury. Copyright © 1953 by Ray Bradbury. Reprinted by permission of the Harold Matson Company, Inc.

The Feminine Mystique. From *The Feminine Mystique* by Betty Friedan. Reprinted by permission of W. W. Norton & Company, Inc. Copyright © 1963 by Betty Friedan.

Curbing Cab Crime in Chicago by John Palcewski. Reprinted from *Olin* magazine of the Olin Corporation with permission.

Virtuoso by Herbert Goldstone. Copyright © 1952 by Mercury Press, Inc. Reprinted from *The Magazine of Fantasy and Science Fiction* with the permission of the author.

First Flight Across America by Ray Helminiak. From *Northliner,* the inflight magazine of North Central Airlines. Reprinted with their permission.

Contents

1 | Introductory Selection

Explains How the Text is Organized and
How to Use It to Maximum Advantage

Vocabulary—The five words below are from the story you are about to read. Study the words and their meanings. Then complete the ten sentences that follow, using one of the five words to fill in the blank in each sentence. Mark your answer by writing the letter of the word on the line before the sentence. Check your answers in the Answer Key on page 106.

A. intent: purpose

B. distribution: arrangement; organization

C. consecutively: in order; one after another

D. corresponding: matching

E. efficient: performing a task easily and skillfully

_____ 1. A wide _____ of topics is needed in order to appeal to all readers.

_____ 2. If you read each chapter _____ , you will understand the lessons more easily.

_____ 3. As you work through each selection, you will become more _____ at analyzing written material.

_____ 4. After finishing the book, you will have a good grasp of its _____ .

_____ 5. The skilled reader has learned that each kind of reading matter demands a _____ reading technique.

_____ 6. The exercises cover a wide _____ of reading and study skills.

_____ 7. In order to be an _____ reader, you must sharpen your critical reading skills.

_____ 8. To communicate with their readers is the _____ of all authors.

_____ 9. Answer the vocabulary questions by writing the letter _____ to the correct word.

_____ 10. Answer the questions _____ , and then turn to the answer key to correct your work.

(Before you begin reading this selection, turn to page 8 and record the hours and minutes in the box labeled *Starting Time* at the bottom of the second column. If you are using this text in class and your instructor has made provisions for timing, you need not stop now; read on.)

It was the intent of the editor to find and include writings which show the real world, the world we all have to face daily.

You are using this text for two purposes: (1) to improve your reading skills, and (2) to read articles and selections designed to make you think. Not every selection will be so demanding, however; many articles were chosen just for pure reading pleasure and enjoyment.

These selections span the range of human experience. It was the intent of the editor to find and include writings which show the real world, the world we all have to face daily. On these pages you will read and learn about current problems facing our society: the use of alcohol and other drugs, the struggle of women for recognition and independence, the seemingly unsolvable problem of disposing of garbage and other wastes of industrial production.

Many selections deal with the quality of our environment and possible new life-styles we may be forced to adopt in the future unless we deal now with air and water pollution, population growth, supplying food needs, caring for the homeless and aged with dignity and respect.

However, many selections treat some of the more pleasant concerns of today's older and more mature student. And finally, some selections just make for enjoyable reading.

Do not expect every selection to be equally interesting to you. In such a wide distribution of subject matter there are bound to be stories which will turn you on, but turn others off. Selections which may bore you, and therefore be hard to read and understand, may very well spark the interest of another reader.

A serious student, therefore, will approach each selection in this text with equal enthusiasm and a determination to succeed. This is the kind of attitude to develop toward reading—an attitude which will serve you well for the rest of your life.

The other purpose for using this text, that of reading and study improvement, recognizes reality, too: the reality of today. This text will help you to develop skills and techniques necessary for efficiency in our society.

Included in each selection are two Study Skills exercises. In these, you will learn methods of understanding, critical thinking skills, techniques of comprehension, and many other key ways to improve your reading ability. Both Study Skills exercises are designed to assist you in developing efficient reading techniques. As you read the selections in this book, you will find that often one Study Skills exercise leads directly to the next. It is important to read and work the Study Skills exercises consecutively in order to understand fully each subject.

Today's reader must be flexible enough to choose from a supply of skills one that is suitable for each reading task. The skilled reader has learned that each kind of reading matter demands a corresponding reading technique—there is no single "best" way to read. As you complete the selections and exercises in this book, you will find yourself growing in technique.

Using the Text

The twenty selections are designed to be read in numerical order, starting with the Introductory Selection and ending with Selection 20. Because the selections increase in difficulty as you progress through the book, the earlier ones prepare you to handle successfully the upcoming ones.

Here are the procedures to follow for reading each selection.

1. Answer the Vocabulary Questions. Immediately preceding each selection is a vocabulary previewing exercise. The exercise includes five vocabulary words from the selection, their meanings, and ten fill-in-the-blank sentences. To complete each sentence you will fill in the blank with one of the five vocabulary words.

Previewing the vocabulary in such a fashion will give you a head start on understanding the words when you encounter them in the selection. The fill-in-the-blank sentences present each word in context (surrounding words). That provides you with the chance to improve your ability to use context as an aid in understanding words. The efficient use of context is a valuable vocabulary tool.

After you have filled in the blanks in all ten sentences, check your answers in the Answer Key that starts on page 106. Be sure you understand the correct meaning of any wrong answers.

2. Preview before Reading. Previewing acquaints you with the overall content and structure of the selection before you actually read. It is like consulting a road map before taking a trip: planning the route gives you more confidence as you proceed and, perhaps, helps you avoid any unnecessary delays. Previewing should take about a minute or two and is done in this way:

a) Read the Title. Learn the writer's subject and, possibly, his point of view on it.

b) Read the Opening and Closing Paragraphs. These contain the introductory and concluding remarks. Important information is frequently presented in these key paragraphs.

c) Skim through. Try to discover the author's approach

to his subject. Does he use many examples? Is his purpose to sell you his ideas? What else can you learn now to help you when you read?

3. *Read the Selection.* Do not try to race through. Read well and carefully enough so that you can answer the comprehension questions that follow.

Keep track of your reading time by noting when you start and finish. A table on page 110 converts your reading time to a words-per-minute rate. Select the time from the table that is closest to your reading time. Record those figures in the boxes at the end of the selection. There is no one ideal reading speed for everything. The efficient reader varies his speed as the selection requires.

Many selections include a brief biography. Do not include this in your reading time. It is there to introduce you to the writer. Many of the selections have been reprinted from full-length books and novels. If you find a particular selection interesting, you may enjoy reading the entire book.

4. *Answer the Comprehension Questions.* After you have read the selection, find the comprehension questions that follow. These have been included to test your understanding of what you have read. The questions are diagnostic, too. Because the comprehension skill being measured is identified, you can detect your areas of weakness.

Read each question carefully and, without looking back, select one of the four choices given that answers that question most accurately or most completely. Frequently all four choices, or options, given for a question are *correct*, but one is the *best* answer. For this reason the comprehension questions are highly challenging and require you to be highly discriminating. You may, from time to time, disagree with the choice given in the Answer Key. When this happens, you have an opportunity to sharpen your powers of discrimination. Study the question again and seek to discover why the listed answer may be best. When you disagree with the text, you are thinking; when you objectively analyze and recognize your errors, you are learning.

The Answer Key begins on page 106. Find the answers for your selection and correct your comprehension work. When you discover a wrong answer, circle it and check the correct one.

The boxes following each selection contain space for your comprehension and vocabulary scores. Each correct vocabulary item is worth ten points and each correct comprehension answer is worth ten points.

Pages 111 and 112 contain graphs to be used for plotting your scores and tallying your incorrect responses.

On page 111 record your comprehension score at the appropriate intersection of lines, using an *X*. Use a circle, or some other mark, on the same graph to record your vocabulary results. Some students prefer to use different color inks, or pencil and ink, to distinguish between comprehension and vocabulary plottings.

On page 112 darken in the squares to indicate the comprehension questions you have missed. By referring to the Skills Profile as you progress through the text, you and your instructor will be able to tell which questions give you the most trouble. As soon as you detect a specific weakness in comprehension, consult with your instructor to see what supplementary materials he or she can provide or suggest.

A profitable habit for you to acquire is the practice of analyzing the questions you have answered incorrectly. If time permits, return to the selection to find and underline the passages containing the correct answers. This helps you to see what you missed the first time. Some interpretive and generalization type questions are not answered specifically in the text. In these cases bracket that part of the selection that alludes to the correct answer. Your instructor may recommend that you complete this step outside of class as homework.

5. *Complete the Study Skills Exercises.* Following the comprehension questions in each chapter is a passage on study skills. Some of the sentences in the passage have blanks where words have been omitted. Next to the passage are groups of five words, one group for each blank. Your task is to complete the passage by selecting the correct word for each of the blanks.

Next are five completion questions to be answered after you have reread the study skills passage.

The same answer key you have been using gives the correct responses for these two study skills exercises.

If class time is at a premium, your instructor may prefer that you complete the exercises out of class.

The following selections in this text are structured just like this introductory one. Having completed this selection and its exercises, you will then be prepared to proceed to Selection 2.

Starting Time		*Finishing Time*	
Reading Time		*Reading Rate*	
Comprehension		*Vocabulary*	

Comprehension— Read the following questions and statements. For each one, put an *x* in the box before the option that contains the most complete or accurate answer. Check your answers in the Answer Key on page 106.

1. How much time should you devote to previewing a selection?
   □ a. Your time will vary with each selection.
   □ b. You should devote about one or two minutes to previewing.
   □ c. No specific time is suggested.
   □ d. None—the instructor times the selection.

2. The way that the vocabulary exercises are described suggests that
   □ a. the meaning of a word often depends on how it is used.
   □ b. the final authority for word meaning is the dictionary.
   □ c. words have precise and permanent meanings.
   □ d. certain words are always difficult to understand.

3. The writer of this passage presents the facts in order of
   □ a. importance.   □ c. time.
   □ b. purpose.   □ d. operation.

4. *Topics for the Restless* is based on which of the following premises?
   □ a. All students are restless.
   □ b. Some students learn best when they are restless.
   □ c. Writings dealing with real problems and situations should interest many students.
   □ d. All of the selections in this text should interest all students.

5. How does the writer feel about reading speed?
   □ a. It is a minimal aspect of the total reading situation.
   □ b. It is second (following comprehension) in the ranking of skills.
   □ c. It is connected to comprehension.
   □ d. It should be developed at an early age.

6. The introductory selection
   □ a. eliminates the need for oral instruction.
   □ b. explains the proper use of the text in detail.
   □ c. permits the student to learn by doing.
   □ d. allows for variety and interest.

7. The introductory selection suggests that
   □ a. most readers are not flexible.
   □ b. students should learn to use different reading skills for different types of reading matter.
   □ c. students today read better than students of the past did.
   □ d. twenty selections is an ideal number for a reading improvement text.

8. The overall tone of this passage is
   □ a. serious.   □ c. humorous.
   □ b. suspenseful.   □ d. sarcastic.

9. The author of this selection is probably
   □ a. a doctor.   □ c. an educator.
   □ b. an accountant.   □ d. a businessman.

10. The writer of this passage makes his point clear by
    □ a. telling a story.
    □ b. listing historical facts.
    □ c. using metaphors.
    □ d. giving directions.

Comprehension Skills

1. recalling specific facts	6. making a judgment
2. retaining concepts	7. making an inference
3. organizing facts	8. recognizing tone
4. understanding the main idea	9. understanding characters
5. drawing a conclusion	10. appreciation of literary forms

Study Skills, Part One—Following is a passage with blanks where words have been omitted. Next to the passage are groups of five words, one group for each blank. Complete the passage by selecting the correct word for each of the blanks.

Paragraphs of Introduction

The textbook writer works through paragraphs. The __(1)__ with which he communicates with his readers depends on how well and how carefully he has structured his paragraphs.

In each chapter or article, the writer begins with an

(1)	effort	easiness
	importance	efficiency	effectiveness

(2)   paragraph. Like a speaker, the writer offers prefacing remarks to open his discussion of a particular topic or subject.

We have all heard the speaker who tells an (3)   or two to "warm up" listeners before he gets into the talk. Writers have a much more difficult task—they are not face to face with their listeners, and must do more than tell an amusing story to get the readers ready for the presentation. Recognizing this limitation of communication through the printed page, writers strive to create an effective opening with which to introduce their subject to the reader.

The opening paragraph is called the paragraph of introduction—used as a kind of announcement of what is to follow. Frequently the writer will state the purpose he hopes to accomplish in the following paragraphs; he may offer a brief outline of the major (4)   he intends to discuss; he may merely mention one or two of the ideas the reader can expect later in the chapter.

Obviously a paragraph of introduction is packed with   (5) . Because it offers such a preview of what is to come, it is one of the only two paragraphs read when previewing. In magazine articles and similar leisure reading publications, the paragraph of introduction has a special function to perform—it's used frequently as bait to   (6)   the reader into the account. The feature writer knows that he must capture the reader's interest and attention with just a few words. The reader can expect any kind of interest-compelling   (7)   to be employed for this purpose—it is the skilled writer at his best.

| (2) | introductory | innocent |
| | unusual   ordinary | educational |

| (3) | incident | inference |
| | anecdote   observation | secret |

| (4) | opportunities | barriers |
| | conflicts   concepts | errors |

| (5) | significance | statements |
| | questions   judgment | communication |

| (6) | convince | lure |
| | bore   create | move |

| (7) | indexes | devices |
| | chapters   titles | characters |

Study Skills, Part Two—Read the study skills passage again, paying special attention to the lesson being taught. Then, without looking back at the passage, complete each sentence below by writing in the missing word or words. Check the Answer Key on page 106 for the answers to Study Skills, Part One, and Study Skills, Part Two.

1. The textbook writer depends on carefully structured _____ for effective communication.

2. Recognizing his limits within the _____ , the writer must try to create an effective way to introduce the subject to the reader.

3. The paragraph of introduction is used as a sort of _____ of things to come.

4. When _____ , you should be sure to read the paragraph of introduction.

5. The feature writer must capture the reader's attention with just a few _____ .

2 | The Day I Nearly Drowned

by June Mellies Reno

Vocabulary—The five words below are from the story you are about to read. Study the words and their meanings. Then complete the ten sentences that follow, using one of the five words to fill in the blank in each sentence. Mark your answer by writing the letter of the word on the line before the sentence. Check your answers in the Answer Key on page 106.

A. elected: chose

B. immensity: vastness

C. prudence: caution; common sense

D. humiliating: humbling; embarrassing

E. futile: useless

_____ 1. People should use _____ when swimming in the ocean.

_____ 2. It is _____ to admit you have made a silly mistake.

_____ 3. Shouting into the wind is a _____ exercise.

_____ 4. When swimming conditions seemed dangerous, beach officials _____ to close the beach.

_____ 5. The _____ of the ocean is awe-inspiring.

_____ 6. The adults showed _____ in forming a human chain to protect their children from the undertow.

_____ 7. The half-mile swim to the public beach proved _____ .

_____ 8. The author found herself in the _____ position of being stranded less than 50 feet from shore.

_____ 9. Bob and Ted _____ to take a nap on the beach.

_____ 10. The author was overwhelmed by the _____ of the waves.

A few summers ago I nearly drowned. But I'm alive today (and glad of it!) because of a lovely blond woman who doesn't exist.

It all happened when friends invited us to spend a week with them at Amagansett on the south shore of Long Island. We found bright, sunny weather the day we arrived, but a stiff breeze and unusually high tides. A recent storm had chopped away the gentle slope of the beach and each wave thundered in against a wall of hard-packed sand.

In order for our four children and our hosts' three to bathe safely, we adults backed into the low surf and, clasping hands, formed a human chain. Within that safeguard the children frolicked and when one of them got bowled over there was always someone ready to grab hold.

The youngsters swam in the morning. Then, while the smaller ones were napping and the older ones reading, it was adult swim time.

That afternoon I elected to stay behind for an hour in order to catch up on laundry that had piled up during a two-week camping trip we had taken before coming to Long Island. When I had the clothes flapping on the line I sprinted for the beach. My husband had already had his dip and was snoozing on a big beach towel. I blew him a kiss as I passed him and splashed into the surf. The other members of the party were still swimming.

"You're late!" one said.

"True," I replied, "but we needed some clean underwear!"

A few minutes later the other swimmers said they'd had enough and turned toward the shore. They left me out beyond the surfline, alone. No one worried, least of all me. I was a Red Cross lifesaver and I had swum in heavy surf all my life. Also, when I was in college I had served on the Mississippi River Patrol, an organization of trained swimmers who specialized in pulling the foolhardy out of whirlpools. I, of course, knew and had often taught the Red Cross maxim which says that nobody should swim alone.

But I had frequently ignored this commonsense warning —I liked the feeling of being alone in the immensity of God's great ocean, and I was confident of my ability to take care of myself in the water. Now I splashed around by myself, turning on my back to watch the gulls swooping low over the gray-blue swells.

Then, having enjoyed my brief period of solitude, I started to head back in to join my husband and friends on the beach. I was about 200 feet from shore in 15 feet of water. I flung a look over my shoulder, saw a good-sized wave coming I could ride on, and tried to climb on top of it.

To this day I don't know if I was ahead of that wave or behind the next one. All I know is, suddenly, in a few seconds' time, I was rolled and slammed—hard—against the sandy bottom. I surfaced, now only about 50 feet from

I had just about given up when a strange vision made me mad enough to fight for life.

the beach, angry at the wave and annoyed with myself for having miscalculated so badly. I swam back out to mount another wave, made another poorly timed try, and hit the ocean floor again. This time I scraped my knee painfully on an undersea rock, but I tried again—and was promptly rolled again.

I don't panic easily, but a small alarm went off in the back of my brain. It said something like, "Okay, smart aleck, you are in a bit of trouble."

The problem was that the surf in those last hundred feet or so was just too rough to swim through to the shore. I *had* to ride through it on a wave, but they were churning too violently and were breaking too far short of the beach. The water was still too deep for me to get solid footing and the undertow was so strong it kept dragging me down to the bottom.

"Never swim alone." I had taught that lesson to hundreds of swimmers—including my own children—but here I was, alone and in what could develop into an extremely dangerous situation. I remembered one of the basic rules for surf swimmers: "If you find you can't get into shore, turn around and swim out where the water is calmer. There you can catch your breath and make some new plans." This is what I did.

Back where I started, I had a clear view of the beach and of my husband and friends all apparently sound asleep and probably beyond earshot. No action could be expected from them.

Now the wind was brisker and I was swimming through whitecaps. The waves were higher; the tide was incoming and surging. A short distance away I knew there was a public beach where husky lifeguards were on duty. I lingered a moment, treading water, torn between prudence and pride. The idea of being hauled out of the water by a lifeguard was humiliating—after all, *I* was a lifeguard!

Just then an oversized whitecap hit me smack in the face. I swallowed what seemed like a quart of salt water, and almost immediately I felt a nagging pain in my stomach. I felt dizzy and nauseous and very cold. It was time, I knew, to ask for help—in a dignified way, of course.

Feeling meek I turned around and started swimming toward the public beach, which I estimated to be about a half mile away—not far on a calm day, but quite a distance in heavy seas.

When I got there, finally, my heart fell. The beach was deserted! The lifeguard's chair was empty and there was a big red sign planted in front of it that said, "No Swimming Today—Dangerous Conditions."

By the time I had struggled the half mile back to Amagansett, gasping against wind and tide, I was really tired. When I saw my husband and our friends yawning and stretching and beginning to sit up, my pride and vanity vanished completely.

"Hey, Bob! Ted!" I yelled. "Help!"

But it was futile; the offshore wind was carrying my voice toward South America.

"I couldn't be drowning—not me!" I thought with a growing sense of surprise and annoyance. I stiffened my body into a human surfboard and made another try for shore. A huge wave carried me in nearer, nearer, then turned me over. I was seized by a terribly powerful force and rolled around and around under water. I ate sand, cut my lip on pebbles, felt slippery seaweed twine around my arms, then tear away.

There is no ocean swimmer who has not, at one time, or another, felt the fearsome tug of an undertow, that strange counter-current that push-pulls you down to destruction. Webster's Dictionary describes it as a "current beneath the waves." Far better swimmers than I have drowned in it. I tried to break through it to reach the beach, but the more I struggled, the deeper I got into the pull of the undertow. Now I couldn't get into the beach—and I couldn't get out again either! I was whirling like a stray sock in a washing machine.

I tried to force myself to be calm and remember what I'd been told to do if caught in an undertow: Do not fight against the cross currents. Go limp. Protect your head by crossing your arms over it. You will come to the surface every instant or so. Concentrate on getting a breath then. Signal for help, if you can. An extra big wave may toss you onshore. The wind may change, the tide turn, and you may be carried out of the whirlpool. Someone may come to get you. Hang on and hope for the best.

I did all that for what seemed like quite a long time, but I was getting extremely tired. I knew that even my ability to stick my head out of water and grab a lungful of air wasn't going to last much longer. Despairingly I cast a glance at the beach, which wasn't much farther away than the length of my living room.

I was drowning less than 50 feet from shore. Ridiculous. It was just a short walk to safety, to my husband and children. Now my arms, which had been rigidly crossed above my head to protect it from the rocks, floated loosely by my side. I let go.

"You are drowning," I told myself drowsily. "Isn't it lovely?" The thought which had seemed so terrifying now seemed strangely delicious. I opened my eyes and in those blue-green depths something very soft and inviting reached out to me. I had a vision of myself standing in a white marble court explaining things to a large and disapproving angel who seemed to be the judge.

"Your Honor," I admitted, "I had too much vanity." Then I added, "And pride."

Other near-drowned persons have testified to the last-moment flash that occurs as you go down and out. Nurses in hospitals have observed that dying patients suddenly become brilliantly alert in their last few mortal minutes. On the bottom of the Atlantic Ocean it happened to me. My fantasy ended. My mind turned on like a high-voltage computer.

"My family!" the message chattered frantically. "What will happen to my family?"

And in the same instant another very cool voice in my brain supplied the answer: "Well, your husband will be lonely. The children will need a mother. Your husband is attractive and successful; he will remarry—after a decent interval, of course."

"Who? Who will he marry?"

"No one you know," the message sought to soothe me. "But a nice person. Don't worry."

Then suddenly I saw her. She had lovely light blond hair, not dishwater blond like mine; she was ten years younger and ten pounds lighter. And she was standing in the doorway of my house with her arms around my children as she smilingly watched my handsome, adorable husband come up the driveway at the end of a day's work. It was all hers now!

"Why, the hussy!" I thought indignantly. "She's got a lot of nerve! I'll be gosh darned if I. . . ." A burst of pure rage swept through me and with it undoubtedly, a good shot of life-saving adrenalin. I planted my feet on the ocean floor, pushed hard and surfaced, straight up like a dolphin. I found myself face to face with my host, Bob, who had noticed the roughening surf and had come out to look for me.

"Jump!" he shouted as another wave towered.

"I can't!" I gasped. He grabbed me and heaved me over his head neatly on top of the oncoming wave. I was washed up onto the beach like a piece of driftwood. Weakly I crawled through the foaming shallow water onto the dry, warm sand and collapsed in my husband's arms.

Still a bit groggy from his nap, he hauled me to my feet and wrapped me in a big towel. He looked as blessedly solid as a dock piling, and I clung to him. After making sure I was all right, he began to scold me.

"Foolish!" he said. "Nobody's swimming on ten miles of this beach but you. And, besides, you know better than to go swimming *alone*! Who do you think you are?"

"Your wife," I choked gratefully. "I'll have 'never swim alone' tattooed on my. . . . Oh, Honey, I love you!"

Later I tried to thank my rescuer for his help. He was offhand about it, knowing that one lifesaver doesn't embarrass another. "Looked like you could use a tow," was all he said.

And, of course, I'll never be able to thank the beautiful, mysterious blond woman who helped to save my life. In fact, I hope she stays on the bottom of the Atlantic Ocean where she belongs—and that the rest of us have enough sense to stay on top.

Starting Time		Finishing Time	
Reading Time		Reading Rate	
Comprehension		Vocabulary	

Comprehension — Read the following questions and statements. For each one, put an *x* in the box before the option that contains the most complete or accurate answer. Check your answers in the Answer Key on page 106.

1. As the author was drowning, she had a vision of
   - ☐ a. an angel.
   - ☐ b. a blond woman.
   - ☐ c. her own funeral.
   - ☐ d. her children dressed in black.

2. The narrator was a
   - ☐ a. newcomer to strong currents and heavy surf.
   - ☐ b. careful and prudent swimmer.
   - ☐ c. strong, experienced swimmer.
   - ☐ d. former professional swimming instructor.

3. The author first realized she was in trouble
   - ☐ a. after hitting the ocean bottom three times.
   - ☐ b. when she saw that the public beach was closed.
   - ☐ c. while shouting to her friends on the beach.
   - ☐ d. when she felt a pain in her stomach.

4. The purpose of the selection is to
   - ☐ a. warn and instruct.
   - ☐ b. impress and entertain.
   - ☐ c. criticize and frighten.
   - ☐ d. alarm and discourage.

5. Which of the following combination of conditions presents a serious threat to bathers?
   - ☐ a. long waves and a sandy bottom
   - ☐ b. high tides and distance swimming
   - ☐ c. low tides and high winds
   - ☐ d. rough surf and strong undertow

6. The decision to form a human chain was a
   - ☐ a. good idea.
   - ☐ b. foolish idea.
   - ☐ c. calculated risk.
   - ☐ d. childish impulse.

7. The ocean, in all its moods, should be considered with
   - ☐ a. fear.
   - ☐ b. respect.
   - ☐ c. suspicion.
   - ☐ d. trust.

8. The underlying tone of the selection is
   - ☐ a. serious.
   - ☐ b. casual.
   - ☐ c. humorous.
   - ☐ d. mysterious.

9. Bob was
   - ☐ a. considerate.
   - ☐ b. forgetful.
   - ☐ c. timid.
   - ☐ d. indecisive.

10. Two examples of alliteration can be found in the selection:
   - ☐ a. chattered frantically, thought indignantly
   - ☐ b. hard-packed sand, gray-blue swells
   - ☐ c. rigidly crossed, promptly rolled
   - ☐ d. vanity vanished, mortal minutes

Comprehension Skills

1. recalling specific facts	6. making a judgment
2. retaining concepts	7. making an inference
3. organizing facts	8. recognizing tone
4. understanding the main idea	9. understanding characters
5. drawing a conclusion	10. appreciation of literary forms

Study Skills, Part One — Following is a passage with blanks where words have been omitted. Next to the passage are groups of five words, one group for each blank. Complete the passage by selecting the correct word for each of the blanks.

Paragraphs of Illustration

As the name suggests, paragraphs of illustration present examples, illustrations, stories, anecdotes, and so on. They are used by the author to illustrate, clarify, demonstrate, or amplify some idea or concept for the reader. Authors use many paragraphs of illustration to help the reader ___(1)___ the subject.

These paragraphs are also easy to recognize and identify because of the use of key words and phrases like "For example," "An illustration of this," "By way of illustration," and so on. These and ___(2)___ phrases tell the reader that an example or illustrative story is coming up.

Surprisingly, half a chapter, lesson, or article may be ___(3)___ of paragraphs of illustration. Unlike lecturers who

(1)   consider   reject
    approve   change   understand

(2)   simpler   similar
    familiar   singular   unusual

(3)   devoid   disposed
    combined   composed   compared

are face-to-face with their students, the author is confined by the ___(4)___ of print. The author cannot see the students. He cannot tell how effectively his ideas are coming across. Because the author has no way of knowing this, more illustrations must be used than would be when speaking. He cannot take a chance; it must be ensured that everyone will get the point.

The writer, too, cannot be questioned over a misunderstood concept; there is no way to pause and ___(5)___ . It must be certain the first time that the student gets it—there are no second chances. For all of these reasons, we can see why much of what we read is illustrative, even in textbooks.

Selective readers are ___(6)___ in their approach. This means that while they may pause over paragraphs of definition, they often speed past paragraphs of illustration. After all, if you understand the point being illustrated, it is not necessary to ___(7)___ over additional paragraphs illustrating this same point. You can move on to the place where something new is being presented.

(4)	limitations		inspirations
	exaggeration	situations	aggravation

(5)	deny		consider
	clarify	reflect	correct

(6)	lazy		cautious
	confused	flexible	careless

(7)	linger		skip
	pursue	ponder	worry

Study Skills, Part Two—Read the study skills passage again, paying special attention to the lesson being taught. Then, without looking back at the passage, complete each sentence below by writing in the missing word or words. Check the Answer Key on page 106 for the answers to Study Skills, Part One, and Study Skills, Part Two.

1. Paragraphs of illustration are used by the author to help the reader understand an _____ .

2. Because the author cannot see the _____ , he is unable to tell how effectively his ideas are coming across.

3. The writer must be certain that his concepts are not questioned or _____ .

4. Selective readers often _____ past paragraphs of illustration.

5. If you understand the point being illustrated, you can move on to the place where something _____ is being presented.

3 | # Killer: Autobiography of a Mafia Hit Man

by Joey

Vocabulary—The five words below are from the story you are about to read. Study the words and their meanings. Then complete the ten sentences that follow, using one of the five words to fill in the blank in each sentence. Mark your answer by writing the letter of the word on the line before the sentence. Check your answers in the Answer Key on page 106.

A. purveys: supplies; furnishes

B. punctual: on time; prompt

C. invariably: always

D. embellishes: adds fanciful details

E. conjecture: guess

_____ 1. A hit man is expected to be _____ .

_____ 2. Joey _____ refuses to squeal on fellow gangsters.

_____ 3. We are free to _____ about why Joey chose the life of a Mafia hit man.

_____ 4. Joey probably _____ his stories to impress people.

_____ 5. Gamblers are not known to be _____ .

_____ 6. Joey _____ valuable information to organized crime experts.

_____ 7. Police detectives know that an informant often _____ his or her story.

_____ 8. Joey _____ certain gruesome services for America's crime bosses.

_____ 9. Police can only _____ about the number of hit men currently working in the United States.

_____ 10. Joey _____ accepts any chance to make a bet.

Joey is a businessman. Over the years, he has held various positions from salesman to collecting agent and company troubleshooter. Generally his organization has been satisfied with his work.

Joey's business is crime. Two of the services he purveys are death and destruction—services that are in high demand in his industry. He is never begging for employment.

I met Joey a number of years ago. At that time he was on his way down the ladder. He turned into the one thing his employers did not like. He is a bettor—a strung-out gambler willing and eager to get down on any and everything: horses, basketball, football, cards, dice, even cockroaches. If it is a gamble—Joey is ready, hand in pocket. He will bet his lungs.

CBS crime reporter Cris Borgen describes his acquaintance with a professional killer.

Today he is no longer quite the sought-after "executive" he once was—not because he cannot perform. That he can do with outstanding efficiency. But he is no longer punctual. The job he is contracted to do may have to wait while he checks his bets for the day. Money advanced for travel may "get down" on the 3rd at Aqueduct. The trip is then delayed while Joey tries to get it back betting the 4th, 5th, and 6th. If he succeeds, then it's on with business, albeit a little late. But in the business of organized crime, late is absent. Joey, over the last few years, has gotten a reputation for being a little absent a little too often. The "jobs" still come, at least they are still offered. But Joey, more and more, would rather go to the betting window than to the office.

Though I knew of Joey by reputation while I was still a detective, I didn't actually meet Joey until after I had left the police department. The meeting was more of Joey's doing than my searching. He had seen a number of reports I had made about organized crime. He thought they were good—but he knew more. Perhaps it was because he knew how much I knew—that he wanted to impress me with how much I didn't know.

He took it upon himself to fill me in. Police graft in New York City? Look, he would say, you're right, but here is the way a pad works. Then he would give me a lesson in corruption that was like a graduate course in government finance.

Never mind who shot Columbo, he would say—better, why was he shot? Again, right on. In time Joey became one of my experts and I could crosscheck his information against others. He was always in the know, but true to that peculiar code that ensures continuity of life, he would never name the names. If I did, he would verify. But he never volunteered names. Joey is not a squealer. He is a stand-up guy. But he has a funny twist. He wants your information to be right. To him, too much of the story about organized crime is told wrong. And to Joey, that

is more of a crime than crime itself. He only murdered men, while too many so-called organized crime experts murder the truth about organized crime.

Joey is now in semiretirement. He'll still "do a job," but only if he needs the money, which is to say if he has lost more than he has won or if a "friend" asks a favor; an important friend—an important favor. Joey was a "hit man." A killer for pay. A murderer. Joey is still one son-of-a-bitch. I don't know how many men he has killed. He says 38. Joey is many things, but I have not known him to be a liar—at least not to me. Perhaps this is because I have never found it necessary to ask him embarrassing questions like "who, where, or when."

In a mellow moment Joey talks of old times. He will mention names, but not so you can make a case. "____'s job was to hit the bastard and leave him so that the others would get the message." The message is invariably the same—pay back a loanshark or stop trying to muscle in on some other crime boss's territory or don't try to move up the ladder too fast. Joey was more a privateer in syndicated crime than he was a member of any particular organized crime family. It is perhaps because he was a privateer that he was so sought after. Not being identified with any one group, he was free to work for all. His operations were coast to coast. His tools—a baseball bat, a sawed-off cue stick, a gun. He, like all craftsmen, had a preference. For him—the gun, a .38-caliber revolver.

What makes a man a killer for hire? I don't know. Put the same question to Joey and he will give you 2,000 rambling words in explanation. He doesn't know either. But that is what he admits to having been—a killer. A man who kills coldly for profit and claims to have no regrets. A highly paid, eagerly sought-after functioning member of our sick society.

Joey is a cynic. He believes in very little, except friendship. That he holds dear. But he is a demanding friend. He demands understanding, affection, acceptance; and he is serious and unforgiving. If you are *his friend*, don't, for God's sake, tell him that someone has done you a disservice. Joey's eyes grow cold, he leans close. What happened, he asks. Once he has the story, Joey will suddenly leave. It may be a day or a week later, but Joey will have done his thing. The someone who did you a disservice has had a visitor who left him with a cracked skull or a broken nose, arm, or leg. Joey is very serious about friendship.

It is easy to say that if time and circumstances had been different Joey could have been a great doctor, lawyer, or business chief. I don't think so. I don't say Joey doesn't have the brains. But Joey is Joey because he wanted to succeed. Perhaps, more important, Joey is Joey because society gave a value to success in terms of money. And Joey found the quick way available to him to make a buck.

He made a buck, lots of bucks. He also lost lots of bucks. But it is over and past he says—and now it's time to talk about it. There is a lot here we can learn about Joey, and maybe something about ourselves. This is Joey's story. His life as he remembers it, explains it, perhaps romanticizes and embellishes it a little. He was there, on the inside, for 20 years. This book then is his personal view of organized crime. I wouldn't swear that it is 100 percent true. I think it is about 80 to 90 percent true. Once he felt he could trust the person he was talking to, he just let it all hang out. Men like Joey don't look for forgiveness, that is an alien feeling in their emotional makeup. Recognition, praise, respect—these are the social-emotional rewards they look forward to. If you ask the right people inside organized crime about Joey, they will know him. Few by sight, the majority by reputation. The bosses know him. They are the ones who hired him. The button men know of him. He was the one sent in to clean up their mistakes. The hood on the street—they have only heard about him. He was something else.

I know him—but not his real name. He has used a lot of names. I don't know where he lives. I don't know his phone number. Joey gets in touch with me. I don't get in touch with Joey.

Now you are going to know about him. He chose to tell. Why? The answer is a guessing game. He chose to tell for his own reasons . . . too numerous even to conjecture about. But there are two certainties. High on the list will be money and ego. Money because he is still a strung-out bettor and a bettor always needs money. Ego? Because Joey, like all men past their prime, wants to know that he was very good in his day—better than that—he wants you to know.

So—yes, Virginia, there is a Joey. And the fact that he exists is the shame of the world in which we live.

Starting Time		Finishing Time	
Reading Time		Reading Rate	
Comprehension		Vocabulary	

Comprehension— Read the following questions and statements. For each one, put an *x* in the box before the option that contains the most complete or accurate answer. Check your answers in the Answer Key on page 106.

1. Joey's favorite weapon is a
   □ a. sawed-off cue stick.   □ c. knife.
   □ b. baseball bat.   □ d. revolver.

2. Among other professionals in the business, Joey was known as
   □ a. a family man.
   □ b. a free-lancer.
   □ c. an incompetent.
   □ d. a liar.

3. Joey's status among Mafia leaders began to slip when he
   □ a. botched an important job.
   □ b. started talking to the author.
   □ c. refused to accept certain contracts.
   □ d. became a gambler.

4. Which of the following best expresses the main idea of the selection?
   □ a. Society is punished by the monsters it has helped to create.
   □ b. There is honor among thieves.
   □ c. Virtue is its own reward.
   □ d. The true test of friendship is to make no demands upon friends.

5. Joey has been unable to
   □ a. concentrate entirely on business.
   □ b. keep up with the demand.
   □ c. accept important contracts.
   □ d. find needed employment.

6. Employment in Joey's line of work does not depend on
   □ a. his ability to meet deadlines.
   □ b. his skill with his equipment.
   □ c. the economic climate of the country.
   □ d. the decisions of his competitors.

7. It is important to Joey that the public
   □ a. receives accurate information.
   □ b. be kept in the dark.
   □ c. understands his motives.
   □ d. forgives his crimes.

8. The selection ends on a note of
   □ a. hope.
   □ b. humor.
   □ c. sorrow.
   □ d. bitterness.

9. A serious flaw in Joey's character is his
   - ☐ a. compulsion to succeed.
   - ☐ b. tendency to drink.
   - ☐ c. passion for gambling.
   - ☐ d. passion for cars.

10. The statement that Joey will still "do a job" means that he will still
   - ☐ a. honor a friendship.
   - ☐ b. commit a murder.
   - ☐ c. give police inside information about the Mafia.
   - ☐ d. obey the code of silence.

Study Skills, Part One—Following is a passage with blanks where words have been omitted. Next to the passage are groups of five words, one group for each blank. Complete the passage by selecting the correct word for each of the blanks.

Paragraphs of Information

The next paragraphs we wish to examine are the ones used by the author to pass along information on the ___(1)___ . For this reason they are called paragraphs of information. These paragraphs contain names, dates, details, facts, explanations, and other factual information.

In a particular chapter or lesson, the reader can expect to find the meat of the matter in paragraphs like these. This is where the author gets down to business and presents the ___(2)___ . The essential terms have been defined and illustrated and now the reader is ready for the substance of the lesson.

We ask the reader to recognize paragraphs of information because they contain the instructional material he or she is responsible for. Here is where the data is found that he or she will be ___(3)___ on later.

In presenting information the author will probably use one of the following methods of development.

1. State an opinion and give reasons. Look for a clue word used to ___(4)___ a series of reasons.

2. Pose a problem and offer a solution. Authors use this method frequently because it incorporates questioning as an aid to learning.

3. Draw a conclusion and then present proof. Actually the proof may come first, preceding the conclusion. Check to be sure that the conclusion ___(5)___ follows from the proof.

4. Present steps in an argument. ___(6)___ here, too, an enumeration. Look for the introductory signal and circle the enumerations.

5. Make a comparison or draw a contrast. Frequently used in paragraphs of illustration, this method may be used to ___(7)___ information, too.

The paragraphs of information are the heart of the lesson. Study them well.

(1)
edition	subject
reader	students	teacher

(2)
aims	conclusions
facts	introductions	outline

(3)
examined	contained
judged	instructed	prepared

(4)
overcome	introduce
produce	prove	deny

(5)
loosely	systematically
ideally	logically	hopefully

(6)
Delete	Reject
Create	Expect	Ignore

(7)
repeat	withhold
deny	restrict	present

Study Skills, Part Two—Read the study skills passage again, paying special attention to the lesson being taught. Then, without looking back at the passage, complete each sentence below by writing in the missing word or words. Check the Answer Key on page 106 for the answers to Study Skills, Part One, and Study Skills, Part Two.

1. In paragraphs of information, the author gets down to business and presents the _____ of the matter.

2. The reader will find data and _____ material in these paragraphs.

3. In a paragraph of information, the author may state an opinion and give _____ .

4. An author may pose a problem and offer a solution, because this method uses questioning as an aid to _____ .

5. Paragraphs of information are very important. One should _____ them well.

4 | Aged Wait in Stony Solitude, but Not for Buses

by McCandlish Phillips

Vocabulary—The five words below are from the story you are about to read. Study the words and their meanings. Then complete the ten sentences that follow, using one of the five words to fill in the blank in each sentence. Mark your answer by writing the letter of the word on the line before the sentence. Check your answers in the Answer Key on page 106.

A. convivial: sociable

B. reticence: reserve

C. assent: agreement

D. sanctioned: authorized

E. credible: believable; plausible

_____ 1. The woman with the red hat seemed more _____ than the other grim waiting-room regulars.

_____ 2. Max Cohen gave a _____ reason for why he chose to come to the waiting room.

_____ 3. The proposed coffee shop would offer a warm and _____ atmosphere.

_____ 4. At first, it seemed _____ that the woman with the fluffy hair was waiting for a bus.

_____ 5. The waiting-room regulars would be happy if the Port Authority _____ their use of the waiting room.

_____ 6. Many old people showed _____ in talking to others.

_____ 7. The Project Find study of the waiting room was _____ by Port Authority officials.

_____ 8. Mrs. Trebony was not discouraged by the _____ of the regulars.

_____ 9. Mary expressed her _____ to the woman with the red hat.

_____ 10. Before Project Find could begin its work, it needed the _____ of Port Authority officials.

Two kinds of people wait in the Port Authority Bus Terminal near Times Square. Some are waiting for buses. Others are waiting for death.

At times transients cannot get a seat because so many of "the regulars" are there: Old people, from about 61 to 90 years old, who have made the waiting room a kind of club. Some come almost every day, to sit and wait, but not for buses.

Most sit alone, in silence. A few read. Some are convivial and gabby. "Once you start to talk to somebody, you have to talk to them every day," one of the quiet ones said, explaining his social reticence.

Max Cohen struts around the waiting room with four or five cigars in his jersey shirt pocket and one stuck in the side of his mouth. He is a very small, wiry man with plenty of vinegar who wears his bristly white hair cut short. He worked for 50 years as a newspaper deliverer and now often comes to the terminal twice a day.

"Why don't you go home, Max?" he was asked.

"What, to lay down and look at four walls?" he shot back. He lives in a small, sparsely furnished room that rents for $7 a week. "Later on, I'll go out and sit in the park, when it gets a little warmer," he said.

To old people whose dwellings are tiny or dreary or places of endless boredom, the waiting room is a kind of indoor park. It never rains in the Port Authority Bus Terminal. The overhead bulbs are as steady as the sun in a cloudless sky.

200 to 250 Regulars

From 200 to 250 old men and women are known to come to the terminal regularly. Many more come now and then.

Occasionally the Port Authority police come in to clear the room, but it is a futile game, the rules of which are known to both sides.

Two policemen arrived at 1:20 P.M. the other day and stood in the center of the room. One of them spoke in a loud, brassy voice:

"Ladies and gentlemen. This here area is for people with tickets only. If you have a ticket, fine. If not, please get up and leave. Now show us your tickets."

There was a shuffling exodus as the ticketless drifted out into the concourse or the public toilets. For several minutes the room was the preserve of the ticketed minority, but within six minutes things were back to normal.

At 2:04 the police came again and, immediately, three old people departed. There was no announcement this time; the blue shadow was enough.

Some old people come and go like characters in a drama, having fixed roles to play. Two are known as

Some are waiting for buses; others are waiting for death.

"the Lovers." They come in separately, meet, sit and hold hands a while, then leave.

Romeo is in his early 70s, a tall, spare man with bony shoulders that seem like pipes under his jacket. Juliet is in her late 60s, short, round-faced.

"You would think they were 16 years old and just in love," a woman said. "She always wears a veil on her hair. He wears a little cap, a couple of sizes too small, and they sit and hold hands."

Some sitters look invincibly alone—severe, motionless, figures in stone.

It was 5:55 P.M. For two and a half hours now, a tall, elderly woman with fluffy white hair had been sitting alone, in a pink jacket and blue miniskirt, gazing straight ahead. Thin lips, painted a bright orange-red, stood out in a rougeless face powdered white.

"Never marry an old bachelor. They never change their ways," a woman in a red hat was saying to a woman named Mary. "I married an old bachelor. Selfish! Leave all kinds of pots and pans. He was terrible. I had to get rid of him."

For more than an hour, red hat ran on and Mary was held to brief expressions of assent.

"Don't forget this town is made up of all the little towns in the country," a woman nearby in sunglasses said. "It's just another little town, except it's bigger. Everybody came here from somewhere."

The watchers are watched three days a week, from noon to 4:30 P.M., by the friendly eyes of Mrs. Stella G. Trebony and Mrs. Mary Butler. The Port Authority, which regards the visitors as a mild form of nuisance, like an excess of pigeons on a veranda, has sanctioned a long-term study of the phenomenon, which began last June and looks as though it may run on for years.

Watchers for Waiters

The presence of the two watchers goes back a little over a year to the point at which the perplexity of Port Authority officials led to a call for help to Travelers Aid, which led to a plea to the New York City Office for the Aging.

Mrs. Stella B. Allen of the West Side Office for the Aging met with Marvin Weiss, the terminal manager, and five others to talk about what could be done.

"They wanted to get them out, but without being too harsh," Mrs. Allen recalled. "We decided we were not going to throw them out. That we knocked off the agenda first."

It was decided to put a table in the waiting room and to let it be tended by Mrs. Trebony and Mrs. Butler of Project Find, 1966 Broadway.

"Two chief terrors haunt the minds of older people,"

Mrs. Allen said. "One is placement in a home for the aged. The other is going on Welfare."

One of the regulars is a woman who carries two bottles of wine in a shopping bag. She comes in and sips on them during the day and sometimes, when she is feeling loose, she stands up and sings "Moon River," a little bit off key.

Another steady sitter, of a bouncy, outgoing sort, speaks five languages "and he comes in and says 'good morning' in all five languages," an elderly woman said.

Some Dress Very Well

At 7:15 P.M., the woman with the white fluffy hair was still fast in her place. It had been almost four hours now.

A few of the sitters seem to have stepped out of a George Price cartoon. Their attempts at elegance are irreparably gauche. Several old sitters are alcoholics. Yet a surprising number, over half, dress and behave like solid members of the middle class, the upper middle class at that.

One man cuts the figure of a diplomat. He wears striped trousers, a dark blue coat with vest, and a black hat that stands out against a thick fringe of white hair. He looks as though he might have been at the Versailles conference. He sits erect, like a man posing for an oil portrait. He does not talk to strangers.

Mrs. Trebony, who still has the soft accent of her years in Savannah, Georgia, offers assistance to any who need it, and will take it.

Most of the regulars are from the West Side of Manhattan.

Mrs. Trebony nodded toward a male sitter. "He's here because he and his wife sat here," she said. "He goes around to all the places where they used to go, hoping she'll come to get him. He says: 'Why do you think she never comes?' He goes every Tuesday to the grave. People say he's crazy. Now, you know, I don't think he's crazy. Do you?"

A woman who is 90 and beyond the joys of living said: "I really just wish I would die, Stella. I wonder when my husband will come and get me?"

"You better be careful now," Mrs. Trebony said. "Which one of them do you want to come and get you?" The nonagenarian has been married three times.

Mrs. Trebony told of an old woman who came at last to the point at which she knew she needed public assistance, a day she had hoped never to see. "She wasn't even getting enough to eat," Mrs. Trebony said. "She had spent her reserve."

The woman held out for a while more, but finally agreed to make out forms for help. "I hoped I wouldn't live this long," she said. The next morning she was dead.

Mrs. Trebony and Mrs. Butler supply half-fare subway cards to those who need them, as often as they need them.

In this city, that is not necessarily a one-time favor. Old people are often mugged, and they lose their half-fare cards with their money.

The elderly know that thieves and purse snatchers lurk in the terminal to prey on the moving crowd, but feel fairly safe in the main waiting room where a thief cannot quickly melt into the throng.

A few months ago an 86-year-old man named August went into a hospital for seven weeks. When he came out, he had lost his rented room.

With residential hotels quoting $14-a-day rates, or $70-a-week, there were terrors in it for him.

Park to Lure Old Folks

Mrs. Allen, commenting on why the elderly fear being sent to a home for the aged or being put on welfare, said:

"They feel that either just cancels them out as a person. They feel that this is the end of them. That's why they struggle so hard to stay independent, 'to be free,' as they put it."

"They can live in the crummiest little hole in a third-rate hotel, with pipes on the ceiling and holes in the floor, but they'll hold onto it," said Elizabeth Stecher of Project Find. "They only need a little bit of help to stay free—just a little bit of help."

A scale model of a vest-pocket park, with thumb-high trees and tiny plastic people, that sits in the office suite in the terminal is management's vision of one thing that might be done: The Port Authority would create a park near Times Square to lure the old folks out of the waiting room. The approach is one of attrition-through-compassion.

It would not be likely to work. One of the attractions of the waiting room is shelter from bad weather.

A more likely idea is Project Find's plan to open a coffeehouse for the elderly in the area. It has already raised $10,000 for this, and is seeking $20,000 more.

At 8:45 P.M., the woman with the white fluffy hair wrapped her black coat around her and drowsed, her head slumping to her shoulder. A policeman walked behind her. Gently he touched her shoulder. "Mom," he said. "Mom, wake up." She brought her head up straight.

The illusion that one is waiting for a bus is made less credible by an attitude of slumber.

Starting Time		Finishing Time	
Reading Time		Reading Rate	
Comprehension		Vocabulary	

Comprehension— Read the following questions and statements. For each one, put an *x* in the box before the option that contains the most complete or accurate answer. Check your answers in the Answer Key on page 106.

1. What is the weakness in the Port Authority's plan to create a park for the elderly?
   - ☐ a. scarcity of funds
   - ☐ b. lack of determination
   - ☐ c. absence of shelter
   - ☐ d. presence of vandals

2. The Port Authority Bus Terminal attracts
   - ☐ a. drifters and alcoholics.
   - ☐ b. youthful troublemakers.
   - ☐ c. the lonely and forgotten elderly.
   - ☐ d. elderly demonstrators.

3. Soon after the police cleared the waiting room,
   - ☐ a. purse snatchers and thieves filtered in.
   - ☐ b. the regulars returned.
   - ☐ c. Mrs. Trebony and Mrs. Butler arrived.
   - ☐ d. Max Cohen began to strut around the room.

4. The elderly's principal fear concerns the
   - ☐ a. loss of their independence.
   - ☐ b. abundance of purse snatchers.
   - ☐ c. possibility of police action.
   - ☐ d. worsening economic situation.

5. The elderly and the Port Authority police
   - ☐ a. do not understand each other.
   - ☐ b. try each other's patience.
   - ☐ c. play a waiting game.
   - ☐ d. openly defy the law.

6. Max Cohen's story illustrates the
   - ☐ a. need for social centers.
   - ☐ b. abusive rents paid by the elderly.
   - ☐ c. quality of life in New York City.
   - ☐ d. privileges enjoyed by the elderly.

7. The bus-terminal regulars all seek
   - ☐ a. their share of federal support.
   - ☐ b. some form of companionship.
   - ☐ c. a return to better days.
   - ☐ d. the affection of their children.

8. The general atmosphere in the waiting room is
   - ☐ a. sad and pathetic.
   - ☐ b. lively and festive.
   - ☐ c. quiet and respectful.
   - ☐ d. lonely and bitter.

9. Mrs. Trebony is a woman of great
   - ☐ a. depth.
   - ☐ b. ambition.
   - ☐ c. convictions.
   - ☐ d. compassion.

10. Romeo and Juliet were fictional characters created by William Shakespeare. Calling "the Lovers" by these names is an example of a
    - ☐ a. mythological allusion.
    - ☐ b. historical allusion.
    - ☐ c. Biblical allusion.
    - ☐ d. literary allusion.

Comprehension Skills

1. recalling specific facts	6. making a judgment
2. retaining concepts	7. making an inference
3. organizing facts	8. recognizing tone
4. understanding the main idea	9. understanding characters
5. drawing a conclusion	10. appreciation of literary forms

Study Skills, Part One—Following is a passage with blanks where words have been omitted. Next to the passage are groups of five words, one group for each blank. Complete the passage by selecting the correct word for each of the blanks.

Paragraphs of Definition

We have seen how authors use their paragraphs of introduction to "kick off" the article or chapter and to introduce the reader to the subject or ___(1)___ .

The next paragraph we are going to examine is the one used to define or explain an idea or concept that is ___(2)___ to the reader.

(1)	title	introduction
	preface	topic	illustration
(2)	difficult	familiar
	new	unnecessary	old

Fortunately paragraphs of definition are easily recognizable. Frequently, the word, phrase, or concept being defined is shown in italics—this tells the reader that the word or words in italics are being studied and analyzed. Certain key words appear regularly in these paragraphs, words authors use when defining. Look for phrases like "We can define this as . . ." or "This simply means . . ." and similar phrases, often including the word "define."

It is ___(3)___ that the reader recognize these paragraphs because what is defined is important to know and understand. The reader can be certain that much of what is to follow may hinge on his or her understanding of the new word or concept.

Students should study carefully each word of the definition because every word is loaded with essential information. The reason for this is that definitions are by nature ___(4)___ constructed. The words have been carefully selected to convey the exact meaning that the concept demands. The greatest mistake a student can make is to hurry past a ___(5)___ . Look at the contribution of each word to the total meaning.

Question the author: "What exactly does this word add to the meaning? How would the definition change with this word left out?" The wise student always pauses and rereads definitions, at least once. No other single paragraph may be so essential to ___(6)___ of the chapter.

Paragraphs of definition often appear in textbooks. ___(7)___ , they are of extreme value to the student.

(3)	essential	evident
	obvious unusual	useful

(4)	loosely	independently
	professionally partially	precisely

(5)	chapter	character
	sentence definition	statement

(6)	comparison	continuation
	comprehension completion	extension

(7)	Conveniently	Rarely
	Substantially Consequently	Eventually

Study Skills, Part Two—Read the study skills passage again, paying special attention to the lesson being taught. Then, without looking back at the passage, complete each sentence below by writing in the missing word or words. Check the Answer Key on page 106 for the answers to Study Skills, Part One, and Study Skills, Part Two.

1. Paragraphs of definition are easily _____ .

2. Words being studied or analyzed are frequently shown in

   _____ .

3. Authors use certain _____ words when they are

   defining things.

4. Students should carefully study each word of the definition, because

   every word is a source of essential _____ .

5. To capture the total meaning of a definition, look at the _____

   of each word.

5 | Lost in Space

by Isaac Asimov

Vocabulary—The five words below are from the story you are about to read. Study the words and their meanings. Then complete the ten sentences that follow, using one of the five words to fill in the blank in each sentence. Mark your answer by writing the letter of the word on the line before the sentence. Check your answers in the Answer Key on page 106.

A. tantalizing: appealing

B. embark: leave; set out

C. facilitate: make easier

D. finite: limited

E. contemplate: consider thoughtfully

_____ 1. A space station would _____ travel to the moon.

_____ 2. The United States and the Soviet Union might _____ on a jointly-sponsored trip to Mars.

_____ 3. The Earth has a _____ amount of natural resources.

_____ 4. It might take five generations before "moon people" would be ready to _____ on a journey to Mars.

_____ 5. Lack of an atmosphere would _____ the launching of spacecraft.

_____ 6. Many people find the idea of traveling to Mars a _____ notion.

_____ 7. It is humbling to _____ the vastness of outer space.

_____ 8. Before rushing off to Mars, we should _____ our other options for space exploration.

_____ 9. Space settlers would have to recycle _____ resources such as air and water.

_____ 10. Someday the _____ prospect of traveling through the solar system may become a reality.

For three decades the East and West have run a steeplechase in space. The Soviets took the lead first, then the Americans nosed them out. In the past couple of years the East has regained the advantage, leaving the West in the dust. No matter who has been in front, however, the effort to explore space has always been as much a sweepstakes as a science, with each side chasing the prize of international prestige.

But in 1987 all that began to change. For the first time since the Apollo-Soyuz handshake more than a dozen years ago, the idea of Soviet-American cooperation in space became a real and tantalizing possibility. Space scientists and government officials—including representatives of both NASA and IKI, the Soviet space agency—began discussing the very serious idea of the two nations coming out from behind the shroud of technological secrecy and jointly planning their futures in space. Their most ambitious project? A manned mission to Mars with a two-nation crew, a collaboratively built ship, and the goal of planting both the Stars and Stripes *and* the Hammer and Sickle on the surface of the Red Planet.

Understandably, the idea had immediate appeal. Who could argue with an undertaking that would double the talent pool of both nations' space programs, halve the costs, and, not incidentally, speed the recent thaw between Moscow and Washington?

But hold on. The proposal does have a flaw. It's possible that the first people on Mars should be neither Americans nor Soviets. Indeed, it's possible they shouldn't be people from Earth at all. Rather they should be moon people. Let me explain.

We could, if we wished, launch a Soviet-American manned mission to Mars within a quarter century, but it would be a shoestring affair, difficult to carry out, high-risk in nature, and without important consequences. Like our early trips to the moon, the project would involve little more than traveling to a new world, staying awhile, picking up some rocks, and returning. Spectacular, but a dead end. With boosters and landing craft built *just* for that voyage, we'd be left with empty gantries and billions of dollars' worth of obsolete hardware.

What is needed instead is not a one-time sprint to a nearby planet, but a slow, patient expansion away from Earth: a long-term program—perhaps taking a century to complete—that would equip us not just for a single interplanetary joyride but for the coordinated exploration of the deep solar system.

The first thing a long-term Soviet-American space program would need, of course, would be a base from which to launch its vessels. We have any number of sites

Perhaps the first people on Mars should not be Americans or Soviets or people from Earth at all.

on Earth, but our planet is not truly satisfactory. Escape velocity from Earth is 7 miles per second; that makes lift-off difficult. There are only four bodies in the solar system—the sun, Jupiter, Saturn, and Neptune—with a tighter gravitational grip and a higher escape velocity. Then, too, Earth has an atmosphere and weather. Storms inhibit launches, and even clear air offers resistance.

What we need is a place that is altogether otherworldly, a celestial body that, though sizable, is lighter than Earth, with a lower escape velocity. It would also be convenient if that body had no atmosphere. As a kindly fate has it, our closest astronomical neighbor is ideally suited for this. It is the moon, which has a diameter of 2,160 miles, an escape velocity of but 1.5 miles per second, and barely a wisp of atmosphere. Less than a quarter-million miles away, it can be reached with present rockets in just three days. It's as if we'd spent decades launching our ships from some stormy, rock-strewn port, only to discover that all along there's been a smooth-as-glass harbor just a few miles down the cosmic coast.

Fine. So let's dust off the old moon ships, fly our engineers to the Sea of Tranquility, and build ourselves a lunar Canaveral. Not so fast. Just as we need the moon to serve as a springboard to the planets, we need something else to serve as a springboard to the moon. That something else should be a space station. If we hope to shuttle between Earth and the moon with the ease and frequency necessary to build a base there, we need an orbiting facility close enough to Earth to be reached with little booster effort but far enough away that its orbit won't decay and bring it crashing down for at least a million years. The station would have to be permanently occupied with shifts of astronauts, whose job it would be to assemble the vessels that would then reach the moon. Such ships could be launched at comparatively low escape velocities (beginning their journeys from above the Earth, not on it) and without atmospheric interference. They could be safer, simpler, and probably cheaper than craft that must embark for the moon from a cape in Florida.

Once we reached the moon, there would be no limit to the ways in which we could use its resources. The moon is a world with a surface area equal to that of North and South America put together. From its raw materials we can get a large variety of metals, concrete, glass, and oxygen. In fact, a moon base that included mining stations would supply everything we would need for construction except water and the light elements: carbon, nitrogen, and hydrogen. These would come from Earth.

Using the moon as our source of raw materials and Earth as a reservoir of talent and technology, the space between Earth and the moon could be filled with any number of support structures—solar energy stations, nuclear energy stations, observatories, and laboratories. Even some of Earth's industrial plants could be put into orbit, to take advantage of the unusual properties of space (vacuum, microgravity, extreme temperatures) that facilitate manufacturing. What's more, the waste products the factories put out could be much better disposed of in the vastness of space than in Earth's fragile and finite biosphere. To service and populate all these facilities, space settlements—each holding thousands of people—could be built, designed to mirror Earth's environment as closely as possible.

Ideally this extension of the human range should be global, operated not just by the United States and the Soviet Union but by the world at large. In fact, as the moon and the space settlements became more populous, international control could be loosened, and the new worlds could become regional self-governing units of an Earth-Space Union.

It may take five generations or more to flesh out such a system, but only then would we be ready to make the most of the next major step: a trip to Mars.

When that project finally did get under way, the best thing for the Earth people to do would be to step back and leave it to the space people to make the journey. Space settlers would be much more accustomed to the idea of space flight, much more accustomed to low and varying gravity, much more accustomed to living *inside* a world rather than *on* one. They would be much more aware of the need for resource control and tight recycling of such necessities as air and water.

When the colonists reached Mars, they would find it rich in the light elements. Using these along with the resources available from the moon, the Mars settlers, moon settlers, and space settlers could soon become independent of Earth for raw materials.

Such economic independence would help speed the next phase of expansion—out to the asteroid belt where hundreds of thousands of small worlds exist, many of which could be carved into settlements or used for further mining operations. And these asteroid settlements—once equipped with advanced propulsive mechanisms operating like giant outboard motors—might themselves be steered into the vast expanses of the outer solar system or beyond the solar system altogether. No one making these long trips would be conscious of having left home, for they would be taking home along with them.

The process of migration and settlement could stretch out over millennia, but what's the rush? Rather than racing into a symbolic, onetime visit to Mars, we should perhaps contemplate this slow exploration of the galaxy, by a process very much like the dispersal of dandelion seeds by a helpful wind.

Isaac Asimov was a prolific and well-known American writer whose science fiction describes romantic adventures about the distant future. His nonfiction works are noted for making scientific and technological material understandable to the general reader. Asimov's family moved to New York City from Petrovichi, Russia, when he was three years old. He taught biochemistry at Boston University for nine years and became a full-time writer in 1958. Asimov has written more than 350 books for young people and adults, and two volumes of autobiography. His best-known science fiction work is the *Foundation* series. Asimov died in 1992.

Starting Time		Finishing Time	
Reading Time		Reading Rate	
Comprehension		Vocabulary	

Comprehension— Read the following questions and statements. For each one, put an *x* in the box before the option that contains the most complete or accurate answer. Check your answers in the Answer Key on page 106.

1. Compared to the Earth, the moon has an escape velocity that is
   □ a. very high.
   □ b. very low.
   □ c. equal.
   □ d. nonexistent.

2. The moon is ideally suited to
   □ a. become a springboard to outer space.
   □ b. sustain human life.
   □ c. house all manufacturing plants.
   □ d. serve as a dumping ground for waste products.

3. According to the author, the first step toward space exploration should be the
   □ a. completion of a U.S.-Soviet journey to Mars.
   □ b. creation of an Earth-Space Union.
   □ c. building of a springboard to the moon.
   □ d. development of the moon as a springboard to outer space.

4. Space exploration should be considered a
   □ a. money-making proposition.
   □ b. long-term commitment.
   □ c. last resort.
   □ d. patriotic gesture.

5. For space travel to succeed, humans must be willing to
   - ☐ a. sacrifice the traditional family unit.
   - ☐ b. make a huge financial investment.
   - ☐ c. resign themselves to a dictatorial government.
   - ☐ d. reduce their standard of living.

6. A trip to Mars in the near future would be a
   - ☐ a. triumph of willpower.
   - ☐ b. dream come true.
   - ☐ c. hollow victory.
   - ☐ d. insult to human integrity.

7. Traveling to Mars is not
   - ☐ a. worth the risks involved.
   - ☐ b. an achievable goal.
   - ☐ c. the ultimate aim of space exploration.
   - ☐ d. any more difficult than traveling to the moon.

8. The author's attitude toward space exploration is
   - ☐ a. enthusiastic.
   - ☐ b. suspicious.
   - ☐ c. scornful.
   - ☐ d. wistful.

9. According to the author's vision, people in the Earth-Space Union would be
   - ☐ a. playful and vivacious.
   - ☐ b. sensible and cooperative.
   - ☐ c. proud and sophisticated.
   - ☐ d. bold and heroic.

10. The statement in the first paragraph that the "Americans nosed them out" means that the Americans
   - ☐ a. beat them by a small margin.
   - ☐ b. became suspicious of them.
   - ☐ c. disqualified them.
   - ☐ d. asked them to leave.

Comprehension Skills

1. recalling specific facts	6. making a judgment
2. retaining concepts	7. making an inference
3. organizing facts	8. recognizing tone
4. understanding the main idea	9. understanding characters
5. drawing a conclusion	10. appreciation of literary forms

Study Skills, Part One—Following is a passage with blanks where words have been omitted. Next to the passage are groups of five words, one group for each blank. Complete the passage by selecting the correct word for each of the blanks.

Paragraphs of Transition

The recognizable feature of paragraphs of transition is their brevity—they are normally short.

As the name ___(1)___ , these paragraphs are used by the author to pass logically from one aspect of the subject to another. Through paragraphs of transition authors show a change of thought or introduce a new side to the matter under discussion.

The reader should be alert to an upcoming ___(2)___ when he sees a paragraph of transition. He should know the author is about to switch tracks and change to a new topic. This knowledge helps the student to organize the reading because it is obvious that the current discussion is ending and that something new is coming.

Transitional paragraphs are valuable in other ways, too. Because they introduce something new, they may function as a paragraph of introduction—they may offer a brief ___(3)___ of the new concepts the author now plans to discuss; they may state the purpose the author hopes to accomplish by presenting the following information; or they may try to ___(4)___ the reader's interest in what is to follow.

In another way, paragraphs of transition may function as a concluding paragraph, ___(5)___ up for the reader the salient points of the aspect being concluded. Or a

(1)	reveals	implies
	injects intends	insists

(2)	change	translation
	correction discussion	persuasion

(3)	suggestion	addition
	rejection condition	preview

(4)	confuse	retain
	arouse discourage	delay

(5)	pointing	summing
	looking closing	opening

restatement of the central thought may be presented to help the reader understand the subject before moving on.

It is this combination of functions and its ___(6)___ to the reader's organization that makes this brief paragraph so valuable.

Because in any well-written presentation the paragraphs have certain jobs or functions to perform, a knowledge of paragraph ___(7)___ is valuable to the reader.

(6)   statement   continuation
   tribute contribution   suggestion

(7)   areas   situations
   conditions conclusions   roles

Study Skills, Part Two—Read the study skills passage again, paying special attention to the lesson being taught. Then, without looking back at the passage, complete each sentence below by writing in the missing word or words. Check the Answer Key on page 106 for the answers to Study Skills, Part One, and Study Skills, Part Two.

1. Paragraphs of transition are normally _____ .

2. The reader knows that the current discussion is _____ when he sees a paragraph of transition.

3. Paragraphs of transition sometimes function as paragraphs of _____ when they state new concepts the author plans to discuss.

4. These paragraphs may be used as _____ paragraphs when they restate a central thought before moving on.

5. The paragraph of transition is valuable to the reader because it has a combination of _____ .

6 **Body Language Spoken Here**

by Elizabeth McGough

Vocabulary—The five words below are from the story you are about to read. Study the words and their meanings. Then complete the ten sentences that follow, using one of the five words to fill in the blank in each sentence. Mark your answer by writing the letter of the word on the line before the sentence. Check your answers in the Answer Key on page 106.

A. intently: with great concentration

B. animatedly: with great liveliness or spirit

C. queuing up: lining up

D. remnants: traces

E. profusely: extravagantly; copiously

_____ 1. In many cities, people can be seen _____ for bus rides, movie tickets, and supermarket purchases.

_____ 2. North Americans become self-conscious when they see someone watching them _____ .

_____ 3. Some people apologize _____ after making an embarrassing statement.

_____ 4. People in Spain are not used to _____ in an orderly fashion.

_____ 5. Spanish boys and girls often talk _____ while they stroll arm-in-arm down the street.

_____ 6. People on the streets of North American cities do not usually stare _____ at fellow pedestrians.

_____ 7. The Japanese notice _____ of class consciousness in the greetings of American businessmen.

_____ 8. In Arab cultures, it is common for men to laugh, cry, and hug _____ .

_____ 9. The excited boy's face glowed _____ during the conversation.

_____ 10. _____ of cultural values can be seen in people's body language.

Like spoken language, body language varies from one culture to another. In fact, many sociologists feel that anyone representing our country abroad should be required to study the non-verbal communications of the foreign country as well as the spoken language.

Whether we're aware of it or not, 70 percent of what we communicate is non-verbal. *Kinesics,* or the study of non-verbal communications, adds a whole new dimension to international understanding.

Seventy percent of what we communicate is non-verbal.

Those visiting a foreign country should heed the comments of one expert in kinesics. "Watch where people stand when they talk to you and don't back up if they stand close. You will feel funny doing this, but it's amazing the difference it makes in people's attitudes."

If people get too close, we—North Americans—tend to back up. We feel they are being pushy and aggressive, breathing down our necks and into our faces. They consider us cold and standoffish. We unconsciously move away. They begin to wonder how they have offended us. Bewildered, soon they have trouble expressing themselves, and often lose the train of thought.

Latin Americans, Poles, and Italians particularly find North Americans difficult to understand in this respect. We prefer to stand about two to three feet apart during conversation.

Jennie, traveling abroad last summer, discovered great differences in body language. In Arabia, she noticed that natives stand very close in normal conversation, gazing intently into each other's eyes. Although no intimacy was intended by this, she preferred to move away. "An Arab likes to smell his friend," Jennie was told.

She found Arab men emotional and sometimes moved to tears, extremely warm and affectionate, often embracing each other. On the other hand, Arab women are expected to be cold and unemotional, almost the opposite of the roles we assign the sexes in our country.

She recalled with embarrassment that an Arab family they met noticed how her father backed away. And whenever they walked along the street, they often saw natives staring at them. "I had the uneasy feeling that my slip was showing," she laughed. In the United States, street behavior requires a balance of attention and inattention. You look just enough to acknowledge the passerby's presence. Look too much and you are nosy—too little and you appear haughty. On our streets, both persons look briefly, then sort of "dim the lights" by glancing down at the pavement.

Eye movements, too, vary from one culture to another. Our normal eye contacts last about one second. Should a young American boy hold a girl's eyes longer, he tips the relationship to a warmer one.

We listen in conversation, with neck slightly outstretched, attentively nodding or murmuring, "um, uh-huh," as our eyes look at the other person. In England Jennie found a fixed stare and an occasional eye blink were normal attentive-listener patterns. Unaccustomed to this, at first Jennie thought her English friend was bored—or just tuned out.

In the Far East it is considered rude to look at the person at all during conversation. Asians also use eye movements which, in our culture, might be considered evasive, shifty, as though one has something to hide.

In Spain Jennie watched two men walk along the street, arms linked at nearly armpit level. They talked animatedly, breathing into each other's faces. Along the Mediterranean, teenage Spanish girls often enjoy the *paseo,* or evening stroll, arm in arm or holding hands with each other. Both are examples of perfectly acceptable street behavior that would surely be greeted with raised eyebrows here.

Habits of queuing up differ in many countries, and Spain was no exception. In church, Jennie watched people mill around, all making their way to the communion rail from every section of the church at once, without the sense of orderliness or lining up, row by row, as we would do. At a bullfight in Malaga, as at events in many European towns, she found people did not line up to buy tickets. Instead, she often saw pushing and shoving, hands waving money at the cashier, everyone edging his way to enter any public event.

A Frenchman traveling to the United States was amazed at our "docile" restaurant habits. "You line up to be seated, and you accept any table offered," he observed.

In this country, most people regardless of wealth or status are served on a first-come, first-served basis. In Europe, where remnants of the class system still exist, many feel group conformity offends their individual dignity.

Japanese consider our status system complex and even humorous. A Japanese described American businessmen meeting this way: "They pound each other on the back profusely, shake hands, and both offer cigars at once. Both men refuse the cigar, more insistence occurs, then finally the man of inferior status will accept his superior's cigar." As silly as this seems, the pattern may not be totally unrecognizable in our country. In Japan, relative status or rank is the key to their way of life. Only there, open acknowledgment of inferiority is common. Our way of "bowing" to higher rank takes more subtle form. We proceed only so far into a high-ranking person's office. The superior maintains his status by keeping his large desk—a barrier—between you and him, as a teacher might do.

By Japanese standards, Americans make friends or transact business too hastily. The tea-drinking ceremony is part of the negotiating game for a Japanese. He prefers to look you over slowly before getting to the point of a meeting.

In some studies of our gesture patterns, scientists have set apart certain movements they consider "courting" gestures, from heightened muscle tone to preening movements. Dr. Albert E. Scheflen, a kinesics researcher who currently directs a project on human communication at Albert Einstein College of Medicine in New York City, observes that Anglo-Saxon women, in normal conversation, show their palms very little. But, in courting, "they palm all over the place, even to covering a cough with the palm of the hand showing." This courting, however, might mean a coming together in any way, perhaps even for business, depending on the context of a situation.

Other courting movements include twisting and flipping strands of hair, as females do more frequently in mixed groups. Men adjust their ties, smooth or groom hair, or pull at socks in typical courting gestures. Male gestures are usually less obvious than female preening.

While cross-cultural body language can help you better understand people of a different land, more attention to this language among your friends at home can also put you on a new wavelength.

Attitudes show in all your communications. You can easily pick out the "pulled in," hunched-over gestures of a shy, insecure girl. Or you see the proud beauty who turns her head and nose aside, chin almost touching her shoulder, as if to say, "I am far above you. Don't touch me." Neither girl communicates friendliness. Many expressive gestures and habits disappear in private. They turn on when people meet.

In a rap session, you might spot people who agree with each other. They often unconsciously adopt similar postures.

Other group behavior worth watching includes the reaction when somebody goofs. How does the offender save face? Dr. Erving Goffman of Philadelphia, a sociologist who specializes in public and group behavior, tells us several rituals exist when someone finds himself "out of face." He can (1) pretend nothing happened, (2) make a joke of it, trying to recover face, or (3) be "acutely shamefaced" and apologize. During that brief moment while he decides which tactic to follow, others unconsciously protect him. They look away to give him time to save face, just as when someone is suddenly thrust into social interaction unexpectedly.

For example, Brian joins you, Sue, and Bob in a booth at the pizza parlor. Conversation centers around going-steady habits at your school. "You know what I think of anybody who would wear matching T-shirts with his girl," Brian quips. "Well, that must be like nowhere. . . ." A body-language signal from you stops him cold. Sue and Bob look at each other, away from Brian. Their slightly open jackets show matching T-shirts. Brian gets the message. He swallows, pulls at his shirt collar (a feeling-cornered gesture). He begins, "Well, what I meant. . . ." Probably you all have a good laugh, depending on Brian's cool. How would you handle it if you were in Brian's place? What one does often depends on the feedback in expressive mannerisms from others involved.

Your expressive signs can qualify everything you say. Suppose you are talking to some friends. "Well, of course, I'm still going steady with Rick," Ann says, as she slides his class ring off and on her finger. A tension-relieving mannerism, this possibly means she is thinking "Should I break it off, and find someone else?"

A public speaker may say, "I love the young people of this country." He spreads his arms wide apart, in a familiar loving gesture. Then he says, "They are better informed, more educated than previous generations." He pounds a fist into the palm of the other hand, contradicting what he says.

A boy with a profound firm walk strides into the room. His aggressive body movements give the impression that he expects to lead the action, or plot its course, no matter what he says. A meek, apologetic boy with a flat-footed or shuffling walk makes us think that he expects to follow the lead of others.

We all rely on clues, hints, and status symbols to tell the story like it is. Communicating with gestures began with the caveman. Yet only recently have we recognized the significance of gestures. Silence, once the refuge of the quiet types, no longer exists. Listen carefully. Do you know what your body talk is saying?

By tuning in to messages you send, you may begin to understand the whole ritual of interaction, of getting along with others. Look closely and you will see what you communicate to others and vice versa.

Starting Time		Finishing Time	
Reading Time		Reading Rate	
Comprehension		Vocabulary	

Comprehension— Read the following questions and statements. For each one, put an *x* in the box before the option that contains the most complete or accurate answer. Check your answers in the Answer Key on page 106.

1. Compared to Arab women, Arab men are
   □ a. cool.
   □ b. casual.
   □ c. sincere.
   □ d. emotional.

2. In the United States, correct street behavior requires a proper balance between
   □ a. affection and aloofness.
   □ b. tolerance and firmness.
   □ c. business and pleasure.
   □ d. interest and reserve.

3. The Japanese like to close business deals
   □ a. as quickly as possible.
   □ b. only after long negotiations.
   □ c. before sitting down for the tea-drinking ceremony.
   □ d. after regular business hours.

4. Another title for the selection could be
   □ a. America Makes Friends.
   □ b. Touring the World.
   □ c. Customs Around the World.
   □ d. People Are Funny.

5. Americans traveling abroad should
   □ a. imitate the body language of the country they are visiting.
   □ b. adjust to the body language of the host country.
   □ c. ignore the body language of the country they are visiting.
   □ d. encourage the body language of the host country.

6. The way people of different countries move their eyes during a conversation
   □ a. confuses their own countrymen.
   □ b. reflects their national temperament.
   □ c. betrays their degree of education.
   □ d. amuses foreign visitors.

7. The selection suggests that body language
   □ a. is used by primitive people.
   □ b. goes beyond the spoken word.
   □ c. is a specialty of Europeans.
   □ d. does not help in communication.

8. The tone of this selection can best be described as
   □ a. sentimental and moving.
   □ b. objective and informative.
   □ c. harsh and critical.
   □ d. cautionary and concerned.

9. Compared to Latin Americans, Poles, and Italians, North Americans seem to be
   □ a. less demonstrative.   □ c. arrogant.
   □ b. shy.   □ d. easily offended.

10. The sentence, "A boy with a proud firm walk strides into the room," is an example of
    □ a. figurative language.   □ c. personification.
    □ b. literal language.   □ d. overstatement.

Comprehension Skills

1. recalling specific facts	6. making a judgment
2. retaining concepts	7. making an inference
3. organizing facts	8. recognizing tone
4. understanding the main idea	9. understanding characters
5. drawing a conclusion	10. appreciation of literary forms

Study Skills, Part One—Following is a passage with blanks where words have been omitted. Next to the passage are groups of five words, one group for each blank. Complete the passage by selecting the correct word for each of the blanks.

Paragraphs of Conclusion

We have been discussing the different ways that authors use paragraphs in presenting their subject and how the wise reader profits from ___(1)___ these functions.

The function of the closing paragraph is ___(2)___ : to give the reader the author's concluding remarks or ___(3)___ words on the subject. The author may do this in one of several ways.

First, although this is quite rare, the author may draw

(1)	recognizing		repeating
	accepting	restricting	organizing

(2)	misleading		revealing
	significant	obvious	unclear

(3)		new		final
	familiar	wise	wary

a conclusion based on the information contained in the lesson or chapter. Authors are reluctant to do this because conclusions based on an entire chapter are much too ____(4)____ to be mentioned just once at the end. We can expect to find the conclusion given early in the chapter and the facts supporting it to follow. It is likely, though, that such an important conclusion would be repeated or restated in the final paragraph.

Second, the author may use the final paragraph to ____(5)____ . Here is the opportunity to give the reader points made during the presentation one last time. In effect the author is saying, "Above all, remember this. This is what it's all been about." These summarizing remarks are most valuable to the learner and a definite aid in reviewing.

Last, the author may choose to leave the readers with one final thought—the central, all-inclusive idea around which the chapter was ____(6)____ .

You recall that when we were discussing the paragraph of introduction, we mentioned that in a sense the writer is like a speaker—using some of the same ____(7)____ in addressing an audience. Occasionally you'll find an anecdote, story, or moral used at the end as a cap to the discussion.

This is the author's last chance to reach his audience. If he wants to leave the readers with a last thought, here is where it'll be.

(4)   factual   interesting
    entertaining   boring   important

(5)   summarize   amuse
       preach   present   introduce

(6)   continued   invented
       developed   instructed   reviewed

(7)   instructions   techniques
    opportunities   suggestions   mannerisms

Study Skills, Part Two—Read the study skills passage again, paying special attention to the lesson being taught. Then, without looking back at the passage, complete each sentence below by writing in the missing word or words. Check the Answer Key on page 106 for the answers to Study Skills, Part One, and Study Skills, Part Two.

1. The paragraphs used by the author to finish his remarks on a subject are called paragraphs of _____ .

2. The reader can usually expect the conclusion to be given early in the chapter and the _____ supporting it to follow.

3. Summarizing remarks are a definite aid in _____ .

4. The writer is like a _____ addressing an audience.

5. The author will sometimes include an anecdote, story, or _____ to complete the discussion.

7 | The Pedestrian

by Ray Bradbury

Vocabulary—The five words below are from the story you are about to read. Study the words and their meanings. Then complete the ten sentences that follow, using one of the five words to fill in the blank in each sentence. Mark your answer by writing the letter of the word on the line before the sentence. Check your answers in the Answer Key on page 107.

A. manifest: reveal; make known

B. intermittent: occasional

C. illumination: source of light

D. ebbing: declining

E. peered: looked searchingly

_____ 1. During Leonard Mead's nightly walks, he often _____ down darkened streets.

_____ 2. In the evening, viewing screens offered the only _____ in most houses.

_____ 3. Leonard felt his confidence _____ when the police car began interrogating him.

_____ 4. Only during the daytime did human activity _____ itself in the streets of the city.

_____ 5. If Leonard had _____ into the windows of most houses, he would have seen people sitting around a viewing screen.

_____ 6. The electronic voice from within the police car made _____ whirs and clicks.

_____ 7. Apparently the number of people taking evening walks had begun _____ many years earlier.

_____ 8. The street lights provided _____ for Leonard as he walked along the cracked, crumbling sidewalks.

_____ 9. On some nights, the _____ barking of dogs disturbed the quiet of the night.

_____ 10. The police car seemed to _____ its intentions when it flung open the back door.

To enter out into that silence that was the city at eight o'clock of a misty evening in November, to put your feet upon that buckling concrete walk, to step over grassy seams and make your way, hands in pockets, through the silences, that was what Mr. Leonard Mead most dearly loved to do. He would stand upon the corner of an intersection and peer down long moonlit avenues of sidewalk in four directions, deciding which way to go, but it really made no difference; he was alone in this world of 2053 A.D., or as good as alone, and with a final decision made, a path selected, he would stride off, sending patterns of frosty air before him like the smoke of a cigar.

There was no one in the front seat, no one in the car at all.

Sometimes he would walk for hours and miles and return only at midnight to his house. And on his way he would see the cottages and homes with their dark windows, and it was not unequal to walking through a graveyard where only the faintest glimmers of firefly light appeared in flickers behind the windows. Sudden gray phantoms seemed to manifest upon inner room walls where a curtain was still undrawn against the night, or there were whisperings and murmurs where a window in a tomblike building was still open.

Mr. Leonard Mead would pause, cock his head, listen, look, and march on, his feet making no noise on the lumpy walk. For long ago he had wisely changed to sneakers when strolling at night, because the dogs in intermittent squads would parallel his journey with barkings if he wore hard heels, and lights might click on and faces appear and an entire street be startled by the passing of a lone figure, himself, in the early November evening.

On this particular evening he began his journey in a westerly direction, toward the hidden sea. There was a good crystal frost in the air; it cut the nose and made the lungs blaze like a Christmas tree inside; you could feel the cold light going on and off, all the branches filled with invisible snow. He listened to the faint push of his soft shoes through autumn leaves with satisfaction, and whistled a cold quiet whistle between his teeth, occasionally picking up a leaf as he passed, examining its skeletal pattern in the infrequent lamplights as he went on, smelling its rusty smell.

"Hello, in there," he whispered to every house on every side as he moved. "What's up tonight on Channel 4, Channel 7, Channel 9? Where are the cowboys rushing, and do I see the United States Cavalry over the next hill to the rescue?"

The street was silent and long and empty, with only his shadow moving like the shadow of a hawk in mid-country. If he closed his eyes and stood very still, froze, he could imagine himself upon the center of a plain, a wintry, windless Arizona desert with no house in a thousand miles, and only dry river beds, the streets, for company.

"What is it now?" he asked the houses, noticing his wristwatch. "Eight-thirty P.M.? Time for a dozen assorted murders? A quiz? A revue? A comedian falling off the stage?"

Was that a murmur of laughter from within a moon-white house? He hesitated, but went on when nothing more happened. He stumbled over a particularly uneven section of sidewalk. The cement was vanishing under flowers and grass.

In ten years of walking by night or day, for thousands of miles, he had never met another person walking, not one in all that time.

He came to a cloverleaf intersection which stood silent where two main highways crossed the town. During the day it was a thunderous surge of cars, the gas stations open, a great insect rustling and a ceaseless jockeying for position as the scarab-beetles, a faint incense puttering from their exhausts, skimmed homeward to the far directions. But now these highways, too, were like streams in a dry season, all stone and bed and moon radiance.

He turned back on a side street, circling around toward his home. He was within a block of his destination when the lone car turned a corner quite suddenly and flashed a fierce white cone of light upon him. He stood entranced, not unlike a night moth, stunned by the illumination, and then drawn toward it.

A metallic voice called to him:

"Stand still. Stay where you are! Don't move!"

He halted.

"Put up your hands!"

"But——" he said.

"Your hands up! Or we'll shoot!"

The police, of course, but what a rare, incredible thing; in a city of three million, there was only *one* police car left, wasn't that correct? Ever since a year ago, 2052, the election year, the force had been cut down from three cars to one. Crime was ebbing; there was no need now for the police, save for this one lone car wandering and wandering the empty streets.

"Your name?" said the police car in a metallic whisper. He couldn't see the men in it for the bright light in his eyes.

"Leonard Mead," he said.

"Speak up!"

"Leonard Mead!"

"Business or profession?"

"I guess you'd call me a writer."

"No profession," said the police car, as if talking to itself. The light held him fixed, like a museum specimen, needle thrust through chest.

"You might say that," said Mr. Mead. He hadn't written in years. Magazines and books didn't sell any more. Everything went on in the tomb-like houses at night now, he thought, continuing his fancy. The tombs, ill-lit by television light, where the people sat like the dead, the gray or multi-colored lights touching their faces, but never really touching them.

"No profession," said the phonograph voice, hissing. "What are you doing out?"

"Walking," said Leonard Mead.

"Walking!"

"Just walking," he said simply, but his face felt cold.

"Walking, just walking, walking?"

"Yes, sir."

"Walking where? For what?"

"Walking for air. Walking to *see*."

"Your address!"

"Eleven South Saint James Street."

"And there is air *in* your house, you have an *air conditioner*, Mr. Mead?"

"Yes."

"And you have a viewing screen in your house to see with?"

"No."

"No?" There was a crackling quiet that in itself was an accusation.

"Are you married, Mr. Mead?"

"No."

"Not married," said the police voice behind the fiery beam. The moon was high and clear among the stars and the houses were gray and silent.

"Nobody wanted me," said Leonard Mead with a smile.

"Don't speak unless you're spoken to!"

Leonard Mead waited in the cold night.

"Just *walking*, Mr. Mead?"

"Yes."

"But you haven't explained for what purpose."

"I explained; for air, and to see, and just to walk."

"Have you done this often?"

"Every night for years."

"The police car sat in the center of the street with its radio throat faintly humming.

"Well, Mr. Mead," it said.

"Is that all?" he asked politely.

"Yes," said the voice. "Here." There was a sigh, a pop. The back door of the police car sprang wide. "Get in."

"Wait a minute, I haven't done anything!"

"Get in."

"I protest!"

"Mr. Mead."

He walked like a man suddenly drunk. As he passed the front window of the car he looked in. As he had expected, there was no one in the front seat, no one in the car at all.

"Get in."

He put his hand to the door and peered into the back seat, which was a little cell, a little black jail with bars. It smelled of riveted steel. It smelled of harsh antiseptic; it smelled too clean and hard and metallic. There was nothing soft there.

"Now if you had a wife to give you an alibi," said the iron voice. "But—"

"Where are you taking me?"

The car hesitated, or rather gave a faint whirring click, as if information, somewhere, was dropping card by punch-slotted card under electric eyes. "To the Psychiatric Center for Research on Regressive Tendencies."

He got in. The door shut with a soft thud. The police car rolled through the night avenues, flashing its dim lights ahead.

They passed one house on one street a moment later, one house in an entire city of houses that were dark, but this one particular house had all of its electric lights brightly lit, every window a loud yellow illumination, square and warm in the cool darkness.

"That's *my* house," said Leonard Mead.

No one answered him.

The car moved down the empty river-bed streets and off away, leaving the empty streets with the empty sidewalks, and no sound and no motion all the rest of the chill November night.

American science fiction writer Ray Bradbury's short stories and novels reflect his deep concern for the future of humanity. His works of fantasy and science fiction combine lively imagination and poetic style. Many of his stories deal with rebellion against society's dependence on machines. Born in 1920 in Waukegan, Illinois, Bradbury has published several collections of short stories and two novels, and has written screenplays for many motion pictures.

Starting Time		*Finishing Time*	
Reading Time		*Reading Rate*	
Comprehension		*Vocabulary*	

Comprehension— Read the following questions and statements. For each one, put an *x* in the box before the option that contains the most complete or accurate answer. Check your answers in the Answer Key on page 107.

1. Leonard Mead had no
   - ☐ a. parents.
   - ☐ b. air conditioner.
   - ☐ c. viewing screen.
   - ☐ d. money.

2. During the evening, the city streets were
   - ☐ a. dangerous.
   - ☐ b. off limits.
   - ☐ c. well patrolled.
   - ☐ d. crowded.

3. The number of police cars had been reduced because
   - ☐ a. the city was trying to save money.
   - ☐ b. people objected to the invasion of privacy.
   - ☐ c. criminals now controlled the city.
   - ☐ d. the crime rate had dropped to a new low.

4. The purpose of the story is to
   - ☐ a. demonstrate the efficiency of a scientifically run police force.
   - ☐ b. show how city streets can be made safe for pedestrians.
   - ☐ c. explain how electrical energy can be preserved in a crisis situation.
   - ☐ d. describe what happens when people lose control over their government.

5. The police car was operated by
   - ☐ a. two policemen.
   - ☐ b. remote control.
   - ☐ c. a phantom policeman.
   - ☐ d. a skeletal force.

6. Which of the following best indicates how different Mr. Mead was from everyone else.
   - ☐ a. He was a former writer.
   - ☐ b. He was not married.
   - ☐ c. He did not own a viewing screen.
   - ☐ d. He was an old man.

7. The city described by the author seems to be maintained and controlled by
   - ☐ a. an impersonal authority.
   - ☐ b. an efficient police force.
   - ☐ c. a power from outer space.
   - ☐ d. an indifferent citizen's council.

8. The tone of the story is
   - ☐ a. annoying.
   - ☐ b. terrifying.
   - ☐ c. encouraging.
   - ☐ d. amusing.

9. Mr. Leonard Mead is
   - ☐ a. representative of the general public.
   - ☐ b. a threat to law and order.
   - ☐ c. an exception to the general rule.
   - ☐ d. suffering from a severe mental disorder.

10. The story is an example of
   - ☐ a. high adventure.
   - ☐ b. science fiction.
   - ☐ c. nonfiction.
   - ☐ d. biographical writing.

Comprehension Skills

1. recalling specific facts	*6. making a judgment*
2. retaining concepts	*7. making an inference*
3. organizing facts	*8. recognizing tone*
4. understanding the main idea	*9. understanding characters*
5. drawing a conclusion	*10. appreciation of literary forms*

Study Skills, Part One—Following is a passage with blanks where words have been omitted. Next to the passage are groups of five words, one group for each blank. Complete the passage by selecting the correct word for each of the blanks.

Inflexible Readers

If the reading habits of most of today's adults were to be ___(1)___, the single adjective *inflexible* would be the most appropriate description.

To illustrate what is meant by inflexible reading, take the situation that most doctors find themselves in. All of their school years and much of their adult lives have been

(1)   approached   questioned   described   withheld   approved

spent ___(2)___ vitally important materials. Doctors must understand the content of textbooks and journals thoroughly. No dedicated medical practitioner is satisfied with less than 100 percent comprehension. Accordingly, medical students develop an appropriate reading skill—a thorough, slow, and careful technique leading to ___(3)___ of many critically important details. The problem comes later, after medical school, when the doctor wants to settle down for an evening's enjoyment with a good novel. Most novels don't require the painstaking attention to detail that a medical text demands. But because of habits formed during years of study, the doctor has become an inflexible reader and ___(4)___ intensively through whatever kind of reading material that comes to hand.

Medicine isn't the only profession that demands this technique. Lawyers, scientists, and engineers tend to read everything in the specialized way that is used to read professional texts.

Another factor leading to inflexibility can be found in the way we are first taught to read. Most of us were required to read ___(5)___ from our beginning texts. By listening to us read, teachers could evaluate our ___(6)___ and see how well we were learning to recognize, identify, and understand words. Our parents, too, could tell how we were doing by listening to us read.

But as beginning readers, we often learn other things at the same time: we are taught to read slowly and to pronounce words carefully, we are taught not to skip words, and we are conditioned to read in this one acceptable fashion. So, as we learn to read, the ___(7)___ that will later make us inflexible readers are being established.

| (2) | avoiding | misusing |
| | ignoring | questioning | studying |

| (3) | mastery | discovery |
| | progress | exposure | theory |

| (4) | plods | races |
| | skips | plots | reacts |

| (5) | silently | aloud |
| | intently | quickly | freely |

| (6) | attitude | poise |
| | interest | progress | sincerity |

| (7) | impressions | customs |
| | habits | text | studies |

Study Skills, Part Two—Read the study skills passage again, paying special attention to the lesson being taught. Then, without looking back at the passage, complete each sentence below by writing in the missing word or words. Check the Answer Key on page 107 for the answers to Study Skills, Part One, and Study Skills, Part Two.

1. A word that can be used to describe the reading habits of many adults

   is _____ .

2. No dedicated doctor is satisfied with less than _____ comprehension.

3. Many professional people tend to read everything in a _____ way.

4. Another reason for inflexibility can be found in the way we were

   _____ to read.

5. As beginners, we are _____ to read in one acceptable fashion.

8 The Feminine Mystique

by Betty Friedan

Vocabulary—The five words below are from the story you are about to read. Study the words and their meanings. Then complete the ten sentences that follow, using one of the five words to fill in the blank in each sentence. Mark your answer by writing the letter of the word on the line before the sentence. Check your answers in the Answer Key on page 107.

A. horizons: boundaries; areas of experience

B. alien: unfamiliar; foreign

C. hostile: unfriendly; antagonistic

D. rejuvenating: restoring youthful feeling

E. savor: enjoy; relish

_____ 1. Finding work that she enjoys can be a _____ experience for an older woman.

_____ 2. Young women today have broader _____ than did women in the 1940s.

_____ 3. For some women, the thought of pursuing a career at the expense of a family is an _____ idea.

_____ 4. Young women should _____ their college years as a time of personal and intellectual growth.

_____ 5. The New England doctor's wife felt penned in by the narrow _____ of her life as a wife and mother.

_____ 6. The Smith seniors who were single seemed _____ toward those with engagement rings.

_____ 7. As a college student, the author did not _____ the prospect of making decisions about her future.

_____ 8. Some career women receive _____ glances from frustrated housewives.

_____ 9. Some middle-aged women return to school for the _____ company of bright, talented, ambitious young college students.

_____ 10. Strangers to the big city often find it to be an _____ environment.

I discovered a strange thing, interviewing women of my own generation over the past ten years. When we were growing up, many of us could not see ourselves beyond the age of twenty-one. We had no image of our own future, of ourselves as women.

I remember the stillness of a spring afternoon on the Smith campus in 1942, when I came to a frightening dead end in my own vision of the future. A few days earlier, I had received a notice that I had won a graduate fellowship. During the congratulations, underneath my excitement, I felt a strange uneasiness; there was a question that I did not want to think about.

"Is this really what I want to be?" The question shut me off, cold and alone, from the girls talking and studying on the sunny hillside behind the college house. I thought I was going to be a psychologist. But if I wasn't sure, what did I want to be? I felt the future closing in—and I could not see myself in it at all. I had no image of myself, stretching beyond college. I had come at seventeen from a Midwestern town, an unsure girl; the wide horizons of the world and the life of the mind had been opened to me. I had begun to know who I was and what I wanted to do. I could not go back now. I could not go home again, to the life of my mother and the women of our town, bound to home, bridge, shopping, children, husband, charity, clothes. But now that the time had come to make my own future, to take the deciding step, I suddenly did not know what I wanted to be.

I took the fellowship, but the next spring, under the alien California sun of another campus, the question came again, and I could not put it out of my mind. I had won another fellowship that would have committed me to research for my doctorate, to a career as a professional psychologist. "Is this really what I want to be?" The decision now truly terrified me. I lived in a terror of indecision for days, unable to think of anything else.

The question was not important, I told myself. No question was important to me that year but love. We walked in the Berkeley hills and a boy said: "Nothing can come of this, between us. I'll never win a fellowship like yours." Did I think I would be choosing, irrevocably, the cold loneliness of that afternoon if I went on? I gave up the fellowship, in relief. But for years afterward, I could not read a word of the science that once I had thought of as my future life's work; the reminder of its loss was too painful.

I never could explain, hardly knew myself, why I gave up this career. I lived in the present, working on newspapers with no particular plan. I married, had children, lived according to the feminine mystique as a suburban housewife. But still the question haunted me. I could

American women of every class and color are all victims of the feminine mystique.

sense no purpose in my life. I could find no peace, until I finally faced it and worked out my own answer.

I discovered, talking to Smith seniors, that the question is no less terrifying to girls today. Only they answer it now in a way that my generation found, after half a lifetime, not to be an answer at all. These girls, mostly seniors, were sitting in the living room of the college house, having coffee. It was not too different from such an evening when I was a senior, except that many more of the girls wore rings on their left hands. I asked the ones around me what they planned to be. The engaged ones spoke of weddings, apartments, getting a job as a secretary while husband finished school. The others, after a hostile silence, gave vague answers about this job or that, graduate study, but no one had any real plans. A blonde with a ponytail asked me the next day if I had believed the things they had said. "None of it was true," she told me. "We don't like to be asked what we want to do. None of us know. None of us even like to think about it. The ones who are going to be married right away are the lucky ones. They don't have to think about it."

But I noticed that night that many of the engaged girls, sitting silently around the fire while I asked the others about jobs, had also seemed angry about something. "They don't want to think about not going on," my ponytailed informant said. "They know they're not going to use their education. They'll be wives and mothers. You can say you're going to keep on reading and be interested in the community. But that's not the same. You won't really go on. It's a disappointment to know you're going to stop now, and not go on and use it."

In counterpoint, I heard the words of a woman, fifteen years after she left college, a doctor's wife, mother of three, who said over coffee in her New England kitchen:

> The tragedy was, nobody ever looked us in the eye and said you have to decide what you want to do with your life, besides being your husband's wife and children's mother. I never thought it through until I was thirty-six, and my husband was so busy with his practice that he couldn't entertain me every night. The three boys were in school all day. I kept on trying to have babies despite an Rh discrepancy. After two miscarriages, they said I must stop. I thought that my own growth and evolution were over. I always knew as a child that I was going to grow up and go to college, and then get married, and that's as far as a girl has to think. After that, your husband determines and fills your life. It wasn't until I got so lonely as the doctor's wife and kept screaming at the kids because they didn't fill my life that I realized I had to make my own life. I still had to decide what I wanted to be. I hadn't finished evolving at all. But it took me ten years to think it through.

The feminine mystique permits, even encourages, women to ignore the question of their identity. The mystique says they can answer the question "Who am I?" by saying "Tom's wife . . . Mary's mother." But I don't think the mystique would have such power over American women if they did not fear to face this terrifying blank which makes them unable to see themselves after twenty-one. The truth is—and how long it has been true, I'm not sure, but it was true in my generation and it is true of girls growing up today—an American woman no longer has a private image to tell her who she is, or can be, or wants to be.

The public image, in the magazines and television commercials, is designed to sell washing machines, cake mixes, deodorants, detergents, rejuvenating face creams, hair tints. But the power of that image, on which companies spend millions of dollars for television time and ad space, comes from this: American women no longer know who they are. They are sorely in need of a new image to help them find their identity. As the motivational researchers keep telling the advertisers, American women are so unsure of who they should be that they look to this glossy public image to decide every detail of their lives. They look for the image they will no longer take from their mothers.

In my generation, many of us knew that we did not want to be like our mothers, even when we loved them. We could not help but see their disappointment. Did we understand, or only resent, the sadness, the emptiness, that made them hold too fast to us, try to live our lives, run our fathers' lives, spend their days shopping or yearning for things that never seemed to satisfy them, no matter how much money they cost? Strangely, many

mothers who loved their daughters—and mine was one—did not want their daughters to grow up like them either. They knew we needed something more.

But even if they urged, insisted, fought to help us educate ourselves, even if they talked with yearning of careers that were not open to them, they could not give us an image of what we could be. They could only tell us that their lives were too empty, tied to home; that children, cooking, clothes, bridge, and charities were not enough. A mother might tell her daughter, spell it out, "Don't be just a housewife like me." But that daughter, sensing that her mother was too frustrated to savor the love of her husband and children, might feel: "I will succeed where my mother failed, I will fulfill myself as a woman," and never read the lesson of her mother's life.

Betty Friedan is considered a founder of the women's liberation movement in the United States. She first gained fame in 1963 with her book *The Feminine Mystique*, in which she protested that society puts pressure on women to be housewives and not to seek a career. Friedan helped found the National Organization for Women (NOW) and led a nationwide protest called the Women's Strike for Equality in August, 1970. She also helped form the National Women's Political Caucus, which encourages women to seek political office. Friedan graduated from Smith College in 1942.

Starting Time		Finishing Time	
Reading Time		Reading Rate	
Comprehension		Vocabulary	

Comprehension— Read the following questions and statements. For each one, put an *x* in the box before the option that contains the most complete or accurate answer. Check your answers in the Answer Key on page 107.

1. The feminine mystique has
   □ a. a useful contribution to make.
   □ b. threatening implications for men.
   □ c. satisfying advantages for women.
   □ d. a strong hold on women.

2. Many women know what they do not want but are not
   □ a. sure of what they want.
   □ b. willing to do anything else.
   □ c. ready to risk the unknown.
   □ d. allowed to think for themselves.

3. The author finally found inner peace
   □ a. by marrying the man she loved.
   □ b. in a peaceful suburban community.
   □ c. after many years of avoiding her true self.
   □ d. through the accomplishments of her children.

4. A woman's life can have direction and meaning if she has a
   □ a. positive self-image.
   □ b. college education.
   □ c. successful husband.
   □ d. fine family background.

5. The author would most probably agree that success should be measured in terms of
   ☐ a. higher education.
   ☐ b. financial success.
   ☐ c. personal fulfillment.
   ☐ d. public acceptance.

6. The reaction of the Smith seniors to the author's questions reflects a
   ☐ a. need for guidance.   ☐ c. unique reaction.
   ☐ b. healthy attitude.   ☐ d. confident outlook.

7. The author objects strongly to the
   ☐ a. traditional view of marriage.
   ☐ b. liberated view of women.
   ☐ c. popular view of women.
   ☐ d. limited education of women.

8. The author's attitude toward her mother's generation is one of
   ☐ a. admiration.   ☐ c. pity.
   ☐ b. indifference. ☐ d. horror.

9. The author found that women who live vicariously through their husbands are often not
   ☐ a. intelligent.
   ☐ b. happy.
   ☐ c. attractive.
   ☐ d. frustrated.

10. The function of the first paragraph is to
    ☐ a. offer scientific information.
    ☐ b. establish tension and suspense.
    ☐ c. introduce the author's beliefs.
    ☐ d. develop intriguing characters.

Comprehension Skills

1. recalling specific facts	6. making a judgment
2. retaining concepts	7. making an inference
3. organizing facts	8. recognizing tone
4. understanding the main idea	9. understanding characters
5. drawing a conclusion	10. appreciation of literary forms

Study Skills, Part One—Following is a passage with blanks where words have been omitted. Next to the passage are groups of five words, one group for each blank. Complete the passage by selecting the correct word for each of the blanks.

Flexible Reading

A good reader is flexible. His reading technique is varied to suit the occasion. He knows that there are many kinds of reading and tries to become ___(1)___ in all of them. Some materials demand a slow, ___(2)___ approach; insurance policies and contracts are good examples. Light fiction calls for a breezy, casual kind of reading at a fairly rapid rate. Another kind of material permits the reader to quickly glance down the column of print, snatching ideas on the run. This is called ___(3)___ . Let us examine the kind of material it is appropriate for.

SUITABLE MATERIAL

We often run across articles, accounts, and stories that are of just ___(4)___ or passing interest to us. These may be unrelated to school or the job; they may contain very little factual content; and they are very simply written. To read these materials analytically like contracts and documents would be a waste of time. To use our study skills and techniques on them would be ___(5)___ and wasted effort. These materials need only to be skimmed to be ___(6)___ .

COMPREHENSION LEVEL

Comprehension is another aspect of flexible reading. There are degrees or levels of comprehension which are

(1)		useful	skilled
	interested	involved	responsible
(2)		analytical	thoughtless
	cautious	considerate	conservative
(3)		cheating	plotting
	skimming	practicing	reviewing
(4)		important	unusual
	great	beneficial	casual
(5)		appropriate	unwise
	useful	nonproductive	unfortunate
(6)		appreciated	misunderstood
	comprehended	avoided	analyzed

_(7)_ for certain materials. For example, a very practical and thorough kind is needed to follow directions accurately. Obviously we don't need this for reading the comics. Textbooks require the student to remember concepts and to understand relationships. The student, moreover, is expected to use comprehension as a tool for thinking. But simple articles of passing interest require only a temporary kind of comprehension—the kind that comes from skimming.

(7)   appropriate   apparent
     unnecessary   unusual   unrelated

Study Skills, Part Two—Read the study skills passage again, paying special attention to the lesson being taught. Then, without looking back at the passage, complete each sentence below by writing in the missing word or words. Check the Answer Key on page 107 for the answers to Study Skills, Part One, and Study Skills, Part Two.

1. A good reader _____ his reading technique to suit the occasion.

2. Some materials such as insurance policies and contracts must be read at a

   _____ rate in order to be understood.

3. Light fiction calls for an informal kind of reading at a fairly

   _____ rate.

4. Textbooks require the student to remember _____ and

   understand relationships.

5. Simple articles require only a temporary kind of comprehension, the kind that

   comes from _____ .

9 | # Curbing Cab Crime in Chicago

by John Palcewski

Vocabulary—The five words below are from the story you are about to read. Study the words and their meanings. Then complete the ten sentences that follow, using one of the five words to fill in the blank in each sentence. Mark your answer by writing the letter of the word on the line before the sentence. Check your answers in the Answer Key on page 107.

A. typical: representative

B. initially: at first

C. ballistics: the study of the functioning of firearms

D. penetrating: piercing

E. autonomous: independent

_____ 1. _____ , many cabbies disliked the Life Guard partition.

_____ 2. The partition is designed to keep bullets from _____ it.

_____ 3. Cabbies are more _____ than police officers.

_____ 4. The people who designed the partition must have had some knowledge of _____ .

_____ 5. Vern Billings believed the cabbies reacted to the partition in a _____ way.

_____ 6. _____ tests proved the Life Guard partition was safe.

_____ 7. Even Vern's loud voice had difficulty _____ the partition.

_____ 8. Vern Billings is more outspoken than the _____ cabbie.

_____ 9. _____ , no one knew how the public would react to the partition.

_____ 10. Most cabdrivers enjoy their _____ position.

"If you're looking for a cabbie who isn't afraid to speak his mind, I've got just the right man," said Robert Collins, Checker Taxi Company's General Manager, in his office on Chicago's West Washington Street. "This guy will talk your ear off."

We had been discussing a new "Life Guard" armored taxicab partition that was jointly developed by Olin Aluminum's technical services and Checker Motors Corporation's engineers at its headquarters in Kalamazoo, Michigan. Designed as a "robber stopper," the partition has, since installation in the cabs of Checker Taxi Company in Chicago, reduced its reported robberies by 30 percent and has to date completely eliminated physical injury to its drivers. I wanted to get a first-hand look at a cab using the partition and hear what a typical cabbie thought of it.

Mr. Collins told the dispatcher to have Vernon Billings, a driver who has been with the company for over ten years, call the office. A few minutes later Billings spoke to Collins:

"There's a guy here who wants to interview you for a magazine article. Can you come into the office? You can't right away? Why not? All right, when can you make it? Good. See you then."

Collins put the phone down and grinned.

"Vern says that he won't be able to make it until 11:30. He's got to go to court. Seems that he took two men to the police station last night because they wouldn't pay the fare. He's got to testify this morning."

I had over an hour and a half to wait, so I went upstairs and talked to Jerry Feldman, president of Chicago's Checker Taxi Company. Feldman, a young-looking man who slightly resembles actor Tony Franciosa, said many drivers initially did not approve of the partition.

"Some of the cabbies said it cut down on their tips because they couldn't conduct conversations with passengers. But now they've gotten used to it. I think it was just a matter of human nature. People don't accept change of any sort, even if it's for the good. I'll bet if I told the drivers that I was going to change the rates on the meters so they would get more money, they'd be against it."

Feldman said his company has some 1,500 cabs on the streets of Chicago and that there have been to date no beatings, knifings, or shootings since the partitions were installed.

"I don't know anything about ballistics," Feldman said, "but that partition will stop practically any kind of hand gun. We ran some tests, and we found that if a potential mugger were sitting in the back seat, there would be only about 20 inches or so between his gun and the partition. A gun fired at that range just isn't capable of penetrating."

An outspoken veteran cabdriver talks about crime in the city.

(According to an Olin Aluminum case history, a series of ballistics tests were conducted using powerful revolvers to determine how effective a plate of 1/4-inch thick aluminum alloy—the kind used in the Checker partitions—would be. Test panels were mounted on a vise at a distance of one foot. One series of tests used a Colt .45 automatic, firing standard ammunition. This was followed by a series of .45 metal-piercing bullets, and next, a more powerful Smith and Wesson .357 magnum. The tests resulted in no significant penetration by any of the bullets.)

Feldman said the Illinois Legislature now requires all taxis to carry armored partitions. "They passed a law that any city with a population of over 1,000,000 must have cabs with a partition to protect the drivers. And, of course, Chicago is the only city in Illinois with that number of people. What they should have done was just say *all* cabs in the state should use them.

"If you want a really positive statement," he concluded, "I'd say that the day of the mugging of the driver from behind is over."

Before going to Chicago, I had spoken on the telephone to Mr. John Love, vice president of sales, in Checker Motors headquarters in Kalamazoo, Michigan. Love said that Checker Motors, a company that has been in business for 50 years, manufactures about 6,000 cabs a year which are sold throughout the United States. In addition, there are autonomous Checker fleets in Chicago, Minneapolis, and Pittsburgh.

Love said the use of the partition is growing, largely due to the general rise in crime in large cities. "The cabdriver," he pointed out, "is a man who just can't afford to be robbed. Generally, he is a very hardworking individual who is independent and unsubsidized. He shouldn't be expected to have his life on the line the same as, say, a policeman or a fireman."

At 11:30 A.M., Collins introduced me to Vern Billings. Vern eyed Collins closely, then said, "You want me to tell this guy what I *really* think?"

Collins laughed, "You tell him anything you want to, Vern." We went outside and got into Vern's cab. He started the engine, then turned toward me.

"To begin with," he said, "I've been pushing for this kind of partition long before anyone ever thought of them. Chicago is rough, believe me. I've been robbed, I've been shot at, I've been hit over the head. Now, for example, let's say I've got some suspicious character back there—in this business you can smell these guys right off—and I do this. . . ."

Vern turned and quickly closed a 3/8-inch thick window that moved in a horizontal track on the right side of the partition. It was startling how quickly he made the move; I estimated that it took him no more than a second.

Faintly, I could hear Vern talking. "Okay, now you just *see* if you can figure any way of getting to me."

Vern was completely sealed off by the partition—which looked somewhat like those used in expensive limousines. The rectangular window section, made of a material called Lexan, was divided into halves. The right side was the portion that could be opened or closed; the bottom section, which was covered by a leather-like material, fitted snugly on the floor and the sides of the cab. The only opening of any sort was a small, rectangular change tray located in the center of the partition immediately below the windows. I thought perhaps one could point a gun through. But the tray was constructed like a coin return slot in a public telephone—when it opened to my side, the other side was completely blocked off.

"All right," Vern continued. "Suppose I've taken you somewhere and I tell you what the fare is. And suppose you're one of those deadbeats who doesn't want to pay. Go ahead and try for the door like you wanted to get out fast."

I reached for the door handle. Suddenly, Vern stepped hard on the accelerator, I fell back in the seat, dropping the microphone of the tape recorder I was holding. Vern pulled into traffic.

"See? You couldn't do a thing. Right now I'd be on my way to the nearest police station to turn you in."

I asked Vern if he had lived in Chicago very long.

"Well," he said, "I was born in St. Louis and was raised part of the time there. Then I went to Dallas, and on to California. I left California to go into the army back in '42—spent 32 months in China, Burma, and India. I've been driving cabs for ten years. Before that, I used to drive a Tasty-Freeze truck. And I suppose Mr. Collins told you I've got a pretty big mouth."

"To show you what a big mouth I have," he went on, "one time when I was driving that Tasty-Freeze truck through the streets there was a big stink about all the racket we made. There was a machine we had that played jingles. I went to a city council meeting to raise a little hell. I just stood up and told the aldermen, 'Well, you're making such a big deal about all those noisy jingles. What about during election time when you guys go around in those sound trucks trying to drum up some votes?' Know what they told me? 'You're out of order, young man.' But they still didn't answer my question."

Vern pulled out onto the Kennedy expressway and headed for O'Hare International.

"I'm not the sort of guy who fools around. Like I said, you'd be on your way to the police station if you were one of those deadbeats. Why, a while back I picked up a really *good*-looking girl and took her out on the North Side. When we get there, she says she doesn't have any money. So without batting an eye, I take her to the precinct. I'm filing a complaint against her, when a guy who was sitting on a bench comes up and asks me what the problem is. So I told him. Then he says, 'Look, if I pay you what she owes, will you drop the charges?' I say, hell, why not? So he pays me ten dollars. Then he goes up to the girl and puts his arm around her. She smiles and puts her arm around him. They both walk out of the station, just like that."

I asked Vern if there have been any successful robberies since the partitions were installed.

"No, not to my knowledge. Well, I take that back. There was one robbery since these partitions have been put in, but it was the fault of the driver. He fell for a very stupid stunt. What he did, he picked up this girl and took her up to Lawrence Avenue near Malden and she said to him, 'Would you mind driving down that alley because I don't want my husband to see me coming home.' So he turns down the alley like a damn fool and he collects her fare. Then she says she can't get the door open. What does he do? He gets out of the cab and goes around to open the door. Then wham! Out of the shadows comes her boyfriend and puts a gun on him and tells him to turn over all his money. And the girl gets out of the cab and slaps him around a little and goes through his pockets. But that was his own damn fault. I would have never gotten out of the cab, believe me."

We pulled into the airport. I asked Vern what his experience as a cabbie made him feel about people in general. He waved his hand.

"People? The majority of people, you take 96–97 percent of them—if you're decent to them, they'll be decent to you. But you've got that small percent that you can't be decent to because they won't *let* you. And the biggest problem is trying to tell them apart."

Starting Time		Finishing Time	
Reading Time		Reading Rate	
Comprehension		Vocabulary	

Comprehension— Read the following questions and statements. For each one, put an *x* in the box before the option that contains the most complete or accurate answer. Check your answers in the Answer Key on page 107.

1. The Illinois legislature requires armored partitions for
   - ☐ a. all cabs in the state.
   - ☐ b. cabs in cities with a population of one million or more.
   - ☐ c. all public vehicles in the state.
   - ☐ d. cab companies with 1,500 or more employees.

2. The Life Guard partition is
   - ☐ a. bad for business.
   - ☐ b. expensive to install.
   - ☐ c. most effective.
   - ☐ d. generally resented.

3. Before going to Chicago, the author had
   - ☐ a. been a victim in a mugging.
   - ☐ b. spoken with a representative of Checker Motors.
   - ☐ c. written to Vern Billings.
   - ☐ d. been skeptical about the Life Guard partition.

4. Conditions in large cities call for
   - ☐ a. the repeal of gun control laws.
   - ☐ b. a more responsive state government.
   - ☐ c. trained drivers, firemen, and policemen.
   - ☐ d. better security in public transportation.

5. The Life Guard partition has
   - ☐ a. eliminated a few cabdriver muggings.
   - ☐ b. all but eliminated cabdriver muggings.
   - ☐ c. not been well received by cabdrivers.
   - ☐ d. contributed to substantial fare increases.

6. The alderman's reply, "You're out of order, young man," is an example of
   - ☐ a. political maneuvering.
   - ☐ b. judicial justice.
   - ☐ c. responsive government.
   - ☐ d. democracy at work.

7. Even with the Life Guard partition, cabdrivers
   - ☐ a. can relax and slow down.
   - ☐ b. cannot be friendly and talkative.
   - ☐ c. constantly fear for their lives.
   - ☐ d. should never completely lower their guard.

8. Vern Billings's last words are
   - ☐ a. bitter.
   - ☐ b. humorous.
   - ☐ c. philosophical.
   - ☐ d. depressing.

9. Vern Billings seems to be
   - ☐ a. self-sufficient.
   - ☐ b. a troublemaker.
   - ☐ c. antisocial.
   - ☐ d. a fault-finder.

10. The statement that Vern will "talk your ear off" means that he is
   - ☐ a. a very talkative person.
   - ☐ b. an argumentative person.
   - ☐ c. a reticent speaker.
   - ☐ d. a poor listener.

Comprehension Skills	
1. recalling specific facts	6. making a judgment
2. retaining concepts	7. making an inference
3. organizing facts	8. recognizing tone
4. understanding the main idea	9. understanding characters
5. drawing a conclusion	10. appreciation of literary forms

Study Skills, Part One—Following is a passage with blanks where words have been omitted. Next to the passage are groups of five words, one group for each blank. Complete the passage by selecting the correct word for each of the blanks.

Skimming for Facts

Skimming is an art and a skill—it is not careless reading.

STUDY-TYPE MATERIAL

Another kind of material that permits the reader to skim is study-type matter in which the student wishes to locate certain facts or extract ___(1)___ data. Actually this is a

(1)   unusual   specific
       unimportant   trivial   meaningless

reference skill—skimming through a chapter or lesson to see if a particular topic is discussed or covered. When the student finds what he or she is looking for, other reading and study techniques can be __(2)__. Consider this type of skimming a more thorough kind of previewing.

When skimming for facts, here is how to proceed.

1. Read the Title. This may tell you if the author's subject is one that might include your __(3)__.

2. Read the Subhead. Be alert for a word pertaining to your topic. See if the author announces a category or classification that might include it.

3. Read the Illustration. Look for __(4)__ information relating to what you are seeking.

4. Read First Sentences. Look for paragraphs that contain information and definitions. These are the ones most likely to contain __(5)__ data. Skim through these looking for your topic. __(6)__ of introduction may tell you that what you are seeking is coming next. Paragraphs of illustration will probably not contain factual data—these may be glossed over or __(7)__ entirely. The closing paragraph is not likely to help, either.

Skimming for facts is a valuable reference skill and one more tool of the flexible reader.

(2)	employed		eliminated
	enjoyed	reviewed	rejected

(3)		interest	opinions
	ideas	information	technique

(4)		grammatic	inconsistent
	graphic	insignificant	general

(5)		factual	erroneous
	frequent	fictional	technical

(6)		Statements	Indexes
	Paragraphs	Chapters	Books

(7)		re-read	studied
	comprehended	reviewed	skipped

Study Skills, Part Two—Read the study skills passage again, paying special attention to the lesson being taught. Then, without looking back at the passage, complete each sentence below by writing in the missing word or words. Check the Answer Key on page 107 for the answers to Study Skills, Part One, and Study Skills, Part Two.

1. Skimming is an art and a skill—it is not _____ reading.

2. Another kind of material that permits the reader to skim is _____ matter in which the student locates certain facts.

3. Reading the _____ may tell you if the author's subject includes information that you need.

4. Look for paragraphs that contain information and _____ .

5. Skimming for facts is a valuable _____ skill.

10 | **Virtuoso**

by Herbert Goldstone

Vocabulary—The five words below are from the story you are about to read. Study the words and their meanings. Then complete the ten sentences that follow, using one of the five words to fill in the blank in each sentence. Mark your answer by writing the letter of the word on the line before the sentence. Check your answers in the Answer Key on page 107.

A. supple: flexible; limber

B. disregard: ignore

C. assimilated: absorbed and incorporated mentally

D. latent: present but not evident; hidden

E. tentative: uncertain; hesitant

_____ 1. Rollo's first notes on the piano seemed weak and _____.

_____ 2. Rollo _____ knowledge very quickly.

_____ 3. The Maestro kept his fingers strong and _____.

_____ 4. In the end, Rollo decided to _____ his master's request.

_____ 5. The Maestro had a _____ desire to teach.

_____ 6. Rollo's body was not very _____.

_____ 7. The Maestro showed a _____ hostility toward many of the sterile new features of the day.

_____ 8. By the next morning, Rollo had _____ all the musical principles to which he had been exposed.

_____ 9. Rollo rarely chose to _____ his master's wishes.

_____ 10. There was nothing _____ about the way Rollo played Beethoven's "Appassionata."

S ir?"

The Maestro continued to play, not looking up from the keys.

"Yes, Rollo?"

"Sir, I was wondering if you would explain this apparatus to me."

The Maestro stopped playing, his thin body stiffly relaxed on the bench. His long supple fingers floated off the keyboard.

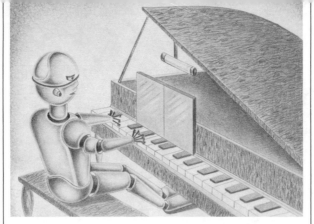

Music is not for robots. It is for human beings.

"Apparatus?" He turned and smiled at the robot. "Do you mean the piano, Rollo?"

"This machine that produces varying sounds."

The Maestro lit a cigarette. He preferred to do it himself. One of his first orders to Rollo when the robot was delivered two days before had been to disregard his built-in instructions on the subject.

"I'd hardly call a piano a machine, Rollo," he smiled, "although technically you are correct. It is actually, I suppose, a machine designed to produce sounds of graduated pitch and tone, singly or in groups."

"I assimilated that much by observation," Rollo replied in a brassy baritone which no longer sent tiny tremors up the Maestro's spine. "Wires of different thickness and tautness struck by felt-covered hammers activated by manually operated levers arranged in a horizontal panel."

"A very cold-blooded description of one of man's nobler works," the Maestro remarked dryly. "You make Mozart and Chopin mere laboratory technicians."

"Mozart? Chopin?" The duralloy sphere that was Rollo's head shone stark and featureless, its immediate surface unbroken but for twin vision lenses. "The terms are not included in my memory banks."

"No, not yours, Rollo," the Maestro said softly. "Mozart and Chopin are not for vacuum tubes and fuses and copper wire. They are for flesh and blood and human tears."

"I do not understand," Rollo droned.

"Well," the Maestro said, smoke curling lazily from his nostrils, "they are two of the humans who compose, or design successions of notes—varying sounds, that is, produced by the piano or by other instruments, machines that produce other types of sounds of fixed pitch and tone.

"Sometimes these instruments, as we call them, are played, or operated, individually: sometimes in groups—orchestras, as we refer to them—and the sounds blend together, they harmonize. That is, they have an orderly, mathematical relationship to each other which results in. . . ."

The Maestro threw up his hands.

"I never imagined," he chuckled, "that I would some day struggle so mightily, and so futilely, to explain music to a robot!"

"Music?"

"Yes, Rollo. The sounds produced by this machine and others of the same category are called music."

"What is the purpose of music, sir?"

"Listen, Rollo."

The wraithlike fingers glided and wove the opening bars of "Clair de Lune," slender and delicate as spider silk. Rollo stood rigid, the fluorescent light over the music rack casting a bluish jeweled sheen over his towering bulk, shimmering in the amber vision lenses.

The Maestro drew his hands back from the keys and the subtle thread of melody melted reluctantly into silence.

"Claude Debussy," the Maestro said. "One of our mechanics of an era long past. He designed that succession of tones many years ago. What do you think of it?"

Rollo did not answer at once.

"The sounds were well formed," he replied. "They did not jar my auditory senses as some do."

The Maestro laughed. "Rollo, you may not realize it, but you're a wonderful critic."

"This music, then," Rollo droned. "Its purpose is to give pleasure to humans?"

"Exactly," the Maestro said. "Sounds that are well formed, that do not jar the auditory senses as some do. Marvelous! It should be carved in marble over the entrance of New Carnegie Hall."

"Sir?"

"Yes, Rollo?"

"Those sheets of paper you sometimes place before you on the piano. They are the plans of the composer indicating which sounds are to be produced by the piano and in what order?"

"Just so. We call each sound a note; combinations of notes we call chords."

Rollo stared straight ahead. The Maestro felt a peculiar sense of wheels turning within that impregnable sphere.

"Sir, I have scanned my memory banks and find no specific or implied instructions against it. I should like to be taught how to produce these notes on the piano. I request that you feed the correlation between those dots and the levers of the panel into my memory banks."

The Maestro peered at him, amazed. A slow grin traveled across his face.

"Done!" he exclaimed. "It's been many years since pupils helped gray these ancient locks, but I have the feeling that you, Rollo, will prove a most fascinating student. To instill the Muse into metal and machinery . . . I accept the challenge gladly!"

He rose, touched the cool latent power of Rollo's arm.

"Sit down here my Rolloindex Personal Robot, Model M-e. We shall start Beethoven spinning in his grave— or make musical history."

More than an hour later the Maestro yawned and looked at his watch.

"It's late," he spoke into the end of the yawn. "These old eyes are not tireless like yours, my friend." He touched Rollo's shoulder. "You have the complete fundamentals of musical notation in your memory banks, Rollo. That's a good night's lesson, particularly when I recall how long it took me to acquire the same amount of information. Tomorrow we'll attempt to put those awesome fingers of yours to work."

He stretched. "I'm going to bed," he said. "Will you lock up and put out the lights?"

Rollo rose from the bench. "Yes, sir," he droned. "I have a request."

"What can I do for my star pupil?"

"May I attempt to create some sounds with the keyboard tonight? I will do so very softly so as not to disturb you."

"Tonight? Aren't you—?" Then the Maestro smiled. "You must pardon me, Rollo. It's still a bit difficult for me to realize that sleep has no meaning for you."

He hesitated, rubbing his chin. "Well, I suppose a good teacher should not discourage impatience to learn. All right, Rollo, but please be careful." He patted the polished mahogany. "This piano and I have been together for many years. I'd hate to see its teeth knocked out by those sledge-hammer digits of yours. Lightly, my friend, very lightly."

"Yes, sir."

The Maestro fell asleep with a faint smile on his lips, dimly aware of the shy, tentative notes that Rollo was coaxing forth.

Then gray fog closed in and he was in that half-world where reality is dreamlike and dreams are real. It was soft and feathery and lavender clouds and sounds were rolling and washing across his mind in flowing waves.

Where? The mist drew back a bit and he was in red velvet and deep and the music swelled and broke over him.

He smiled.

My recording. Thank you, thank you, thank—

The Maestro snapped erect, threw the covers aside.

He sat on the edge of the bed, listening.

He groped for his robe in the darkness, shoved bony feet into his slippers.

He crept, trembling uncontrollably, to the door of his studio and stood there, thin and brittle in the robe.

The light over the music rack was an eerie island in the brown shadows of the studio. Rollo sat at the keyboard, prim, inhuman, rigid, twin lenses focused somewhere off into the shadows.

The massive feet working the pedals, arms and hands flashing and glinting—they were living entities, separate, somehow, from the machined perfection of his body.

The music rack was empty.

A copy of Beethoven's "Appassionata" lay closed on the bench. It had been, the Maestro remembered, in a pile of sheet music on the piano.

Rollo was playing it.

He was creating it, breathing it, drawing it through silver flame.

Time became meaningless, suspended in midair.

The Maestro didn't realize he was weeping until Rollo finished the sonata.

The robot turned to look at the Maestro. "The sounds," he droned. "They pleased you?"

The Maestro's lips quivered. "Yes, Rollo," he replied at last. "They pleased me." He fought the lump in his throat.

He picked up the music in fingers that shook.

"This," he murmured. "Already?"

"It has been added to my store of data," Rollo replied. "I applied the principles you explained to me to these plans. It was not very difficult."

The Maestro swallowed as he tried to speak. "It was not very difficult . . ." he repeated softly.

The old man sank down slowly onto the bench next to Rollo, stared silently at the robot as though seeing him for the first time.

Rollo got to his feet.

The Maestro let his fingers rest on the keys, strangely foreign now.

"Music!" he breathed. "I may have heard it that way in my soul. I know Beethoven did!"

He looked up at the robot, a growing excitement in his face.

"Rollo," he said, his voice straining to remain calm. "You and I have some work to do tomorrow on your memory banks."

Sleep did not come again that night.

He strode briskly into the studio the next morning. Rollo was vacuuming the carpet. The Maestro preferred carpets to the new dust-free plastics, which felt somehow profane to his feet.

The Maestro's house was, in fact, an oasis of anachronisms in a desert of contemporary antiseptic efficiency.

"Well, are you ready for work, Rollo?" he asked. "We have a lot to do, you and I. I have such plans for you, Rollo—great plans!"

Rollo, for once, did not reply.

"I have asked them all to come here this afternoon," the Maestro went on. "Conductors, concert pianists, composers, my manager. All the giants of music, Rollo. Wait until they hear you play."

Rollo switched off the vacuum and stood quietly.

"You'll play for them right here this afternoon." The Maestro's voice was high-pitched, breathless. "The 'Appassionata' again, I think. Yes, that's it. I must see their faces!"

"Sir?"

The Maestro's face shone as he looked up at him. "Yes, Rollo?"

"In my built-in instructions, I have the option of rejecting any action which I consider harmful to my owner," the robot's words were precise, carefully selected. "Last night you wept. That is one of the indications I am instructed to consider in making my decisions."

The Maestro gripped Rollo's thick, superbly molded arm.

"Rollo, you don't understand. That was for the moment. It was petty of me, childish!"

"I beg your pardon, sir, but I must refuse to approach the piano again."

The Maestro stared at him, unbelieving, pleading.

"Rollo, you can't! The world must hear you!"

"No, sir." The amber lenses almost seemed to soften.

"The piano is not a machine," that powerful inhuman voice droned. "To me, yes. I can translate the notes into sounds at a glance. From only a few I am able to grasp at once the composer's conception. It is easy for me."

Rollo towered magnificently over the Maestro's bent form.

"I can also grasp," the brassy monotone rolled through the studio, "that this . . . music is not for robots. It is for man. To me it is easy, yes. . . . It was not meant to be easy."

Starting Time		Finishing Time	
Reading Time		Reading Rate	
Comprehension		Vocabulary	

Comprehension

Comprehension— Read the following questions and statements. For each one, put an *x* in the box before the option that contains the most complete or accurate answer. Check your answers in the Answer Key on page 107.

1. The robot had no need for
   - ☐ a. sleep.
   - ☐ b. a master.
   - ☐ c. specific directions.
   - ☐ d. hands.

2. At first the Maestro thought the robot incapable of
   - ☐ a. error.
   - ☐ b. feeling.
   - ☐ c. service.
   - ☐ d. honesty.

3. To Rollo's question, "What is the purpose of music, sir?" the Maestro responded by
   - ☐ a. crushing his cigarette impatiently.
   - ☐ b. demonstrating on the piano.
   - ☐ c. flexing his fingers briefly.
   - ☐ d. telling Rollo to listen.

4. Carefully programmed robots such as Rollo could
   - ☐ a. never hope to create art.
   - ☐ b. destroy the world in which we live.
   - ☐ c. surpass the achievements of their creators.
   - ☐ d. never refuse to obey an order.

5. Rollo's method of learning is
   - ☐ a. subhuman.
   - ☐ b. inhuman.
   - ☐ c. superhuman.
   - ☐ d. human.

6. Considered objectively, Rollo's reaction to Debussy's music is
   - ☐ a. uncanny.
   - ☐ b. normal.
   - ☐ c. unfortunate.
   - ☐ d. disappointing.

7. One of Rollo's built-in instructions was to
   - ☐ a. light the Maestro's cigarettes.
   - ☐ b. discourage the Maestro from smoking.
   - ☐ c. learn to play the piano.
   - ☐ d. chauffeur the Maestro's automobile.

8. The robot's last statement is
   - ☐ a. humorous.
   - ☐ b. sentimental.
   - ☐ c. insightful.
   - ☐ d. sarcastic.

9. The Maestro was
   - ☐ a. an overtrustful person.
   - ☐ b. a discouraged performer.
   - ☐ c. a jealous musician.
   - ☐ d. a patient teacher.

10. The selection is an interesting example of
   - ☐ a. science fiction.
   - ☐ b. mystery.
   - ☐ c. biography.
   - ☐ d. classical music.

Comprehension Skills

1. recalling specific facts	6. making a judgment
2. retaining concepts	7. making an inference
3. organizing facts	8. recognizing tone
4. understanding the main idea	9. understanding characters
5. drawing a conclusion	10. appreciation of literary forms

Study Skills, Part One

Study Skills, Part One—Following is a passage with blanks where words have been omitted. Next to the passage are groups of five words, one group for each blank. Complete the passage by selecting the correct word for each of the blanks.

Dynamic Skimming

We can label another type of high speed skimming dynamic skimming. We call it dynamic because of the ___(1)___ results it yields at such high speeds. You may have

(1) poor negligible
impressive knowledgeable minimal

seen demonstrations of this type of reading on television or have read about it somewhere. The fact that some reading courses charge fees close to two hundred dollars testifies to the ___(2)___ of this kind of reading as a tool in the repertory of the flexible reader. The steps to dynamic skimming are these.

1. Preview. As you no doubt have begun to realize, previewing is ___(3)___ to reading of any kind. In dynamic skimming, previewing is more essential than ever. Before skimming, the reader must ___(4)___ a thorough and comprehensive preview of the entire article. The steps to previewing do not change. It's just that more time is spent on previewing to form a clear mental outline of the article for skimming.

2. Skim. This time let your eyes flow down the column of print, snatching ideas on the run. Do not stop to read—do not pause to reflect. Strive to let the words ___(5)___ your mind as you skim by.

This kind of skimming is ___(6)___ at first because we've been in the habit of reading line by line. To overcome this natural tendency, use your finger as a pacer to force your eyes down the page. You may wish to move your finger in a zigzag fashion, letting the eyes fixate (stop and read) twice on each line. Gradually speed up until you are able to cover the page in ten or twelve seconds.

3. Reread. This is the third step to dynamic skimming. Rereading is done like previewing, attempting to ___(7)___ any gaps in your understanding of the article.

To be successful, you must have easy material and perform each of the three steps: preview, skim, and reread.

(2)   value   fact
    concept   root   bond

(3)   unwise   optional
    prohibitive   preferable   necessary

(4)   study   perform
    review   predict   anticipate

(5)   trigger   leave
    absorb   open   possess

(6)   necessary   trivial
    difficult   boring   unusual

(7)   read   enjoy
    study   fill   scan

Study Skills, Part Two—Read the study skills passage again, paying special attention to the lesson being taught. Then, without looking back at the passage, complete each sentence below by writing in the missing word or words. Check the Answer Key on page 107 for the answers to Study Skills, Part One, and Study Skills, Part Two.

1. High speed skimming is called _____ skimming.

2. _____ is necessary for reading of any kind.

3. While skimming, your eyes flow down the column of print snatching _____ on the run.

4. _____ is the third step to dynamic skimming.

5. To be successful in the art of skimming, you must have _____ material.

11 | First Flight Across America

by Ray Helminiak

Vocabulary—The five words below are from the story you are about to read. Study the words and their meanings. Then complete the ten sentences that follow, using one of the five words to fill in the blank in each sentence. Mark your answer by writing the letter of the word on the line before the sentence. Check your answers in the Answer Key on page 107.

A. garb: costume

B. infinitesimal: exceedingly small

C. rudimentary: not fully developed

D. precluded: prevented

E. originated: began

_____ 1. The _____ of a modern pilot does not include a cap worn backwards or cotton in the ears.

_____ 2. The name of Rodgers' plane _____ with J. Odgen Armour and his grape-flavored drink.

_____ 3. A series of problems _____ Rodgers from winning the $50,000 prize.

_____ 4. The Wright brothers provided their students with a _____ knowledge of flying.

_____ 5. Rodgers wore the distinctive _____ of an early pilot.

_____ 6. The payoff for Rodgers' great effort was _____ .

_____ 7. The idea of paying $50,000 to the first pilot to fly across America apparently _____ with William Randolph Hearst.

_____ 8. Partial deafness never _____ Rodgers from becoming a pilot.

_____ 9. Rodgers flew his _____ aircraft at a top speed of 55 miles per hour.

_____ 10. From high up in the air, a pilot can see _____ people scurrying around on the ground.

Back in 1911, air travel wasn't too long on refinements.

In September of that year, an adventurous soul named Cal Rodgers made the first flight across America, in an aircraft called the "Vin Fiz."

It wasn't easy, not at all like an airplane trip today.

First off, Rodgers sat outside in a maze of wires and braces, with two whirling propellers at his back. This necessitated his wearing a cap backwards, in the early flying tradition. Goggles, a leather coat, and cotton for his ears were also part of the aviator's garb.

The horsepower rating of the aircraft engine was an infinitesimal 35. There were no such things as windshields, arm rests, or instrument panels. Rodgers's only flying instrument was a string dangling before him. If it hung straight down, the plane was either on the ground or in a dead stall. In other positions, the string indicated with varying accuracy the degree of climb or descent, or a yawing action to the right or left.

In spite of its rudimentary appearance—an open box-like affair wired to 32-foot fabric-covered wings—the plane was the Wright brothers' latest design.

Smoking restrictions aboard the Vin Fiz were nonexistent, so Rodgers's stogie was his constant companion. Describing his journey later, Rodgers remarked, "I could light a cigar with ease at any stage of the flight."

The man had nerves of steel and lungs of leather.

He was certainly equal to the task of being the first man to span America by air. A 6'4", 190-pounder, he was from a long line of American heroes. His great-grandfather, Commodore Matthew Perry, opened Japan's doors to the world. A grand uncle, Oliver Hazard Perry, won the Battle of Lake Erie during the War of 1812. Rodgers's father, an Army officer, was killed before the boy was born.

A childhood attack of scarlet fever left Rodgers partially deaf and precluded the military career he had hoped for. But aviation offered the challenge and excitement that suited his temperament. He attended the Wright brothers' flying school and after 90 minutes of instruction was a qualified solo pilot.

Rodgers bought a Wright biplane for $5,000 and, at 32, began his flying career.

Rodgers entered aviation competition whenever possible and established an American flight endurance record of 3 hours, 42 minutes. At a flying meet in Chicago's Grant Park, Rodgers met J. Ogden Armour, the meat packing scion, who was then marketing a soft drink named Vin Fiz.

Armour was so impressed that he offered to back

I am bound for the Pacific Ocean and I mean to get there.

Rodgers in a cross-country flight. Such a feat would not only publicize Armour's grape-flavored drink but would also capture the $50,000 prize offered by publisher William Randolph Hearst for the first plane trip across America.

Hearst's only rule was the flight had to take no more than 30 days.

Rodgers accepted the challenge.

Armour guaranteed Rodgers $5 for every mile flown, and provided a special train to accompany him. The train consisted of a pullman, a diner, several cars with spare parts, a complete machine shop, and a first aid center.

Passengers aboard the train included Rodgers's wife, his mother, and the Wright brothers' best mechanic. Since there were no navigational aids and few airports, Rodgers needed all the help he could get.

September 11—the magic day—arrived, and so did a huge crowd of well-wishers at Sheepshead Bay, New York, where the flight originated.

"Stand back or someone will be killed," Rodgers shouted as the chain-driven props began to flail the air. His concern was real. The plane had no throttle and the engine had only two speeds: off and wide open.

When Rodgers became airborne, he cut a few capers over Brooklyn at 800 feet. After dropping some leaflets advertising Vin Fiz, he headed west, sputtering along at 55 miles per hour, his top speed.

The days that followed saw a series of frenzied takeoffs and desperate landings, including a nose dive into a chicken coop.

There were endless delays for repairs, replacements, injuries, and a few visits to local cigar stores.

Getting lost was also a problem. Once, Rodgers followed the wrong railroad tracks and ended the day with a net advance of 15 miles.

A big hazard of the flight was the crowds gathering at Rodgers's advertised landings. At Middletown, New York—his first controlled stop—9,000 people were waiting. About 500 autos were parked in a circle to mark a landing spot, but the crowd flooded into the area.

"I had to herd them up before they would clear a space," Rodgers said, "but I came down so easily I didn't even knock the ashes off my cigar."

Other crowds were less cooperative. When Rodgers made a forced landing near Scranton, Pennsylvania, he had a rough time saving his machine. "The crowd went crazy. There wasn't a name on my wings when I started, but in 10 minutes there wasn't an inch free from pencil marks . . . I nearly lost my temper when a man with a chisel tried to punch out his monogram."

Rodgers hoped to reach Chicago four days after his initial takeoff. But things didn't go right and it was 21 days and three mishaps before he saw the Windy City, where he displayed his plane at Grant Park.

At this late date, he knew he couldn't complete his flight within the 30-day period. The prize money was lost. There was no reason to continue—except the pure feat of conquering the United States by air, and Cal Rodgers rose to the occasion:

"I am bound for Los Angeles and the Pacific Ocean. Prize or no prize, that's where I'm going, and if canvas, steel, and wire together with a little brawn, tendons, and brain stick with me, I mean to get there."

He flew on to Kansas City where, according to the *Star,* he gave the populace "an aerial thrill the likes of which it had never experienced before. Rodgers was the first to fly over the city, and he did it with daring, along the Missouri River at 700 feet and buzzing the business district."

Next was Muskogee, Oklahoma, where the newspaper reported, "To those who saw Rodgers alight and step from his machine, there came a sensation as if they had seen a messenger from Mars."

In Dallas, 7,500 people gathered at his landing. On November 1, he was in Tucson and a day later over California.

On November 5, he reached Los Angeles.

Though he had officially completed his journey, Rodgers insisted on flying all the way to the Pacific Ocean. He succeeded, but not without another serious crackup and a broken ankle. (Next day he remarked, "I hit the ground a mighty hard whack, but I'm going to finish the flight and finish it with that machine.")

When he finally taxied his Vin Fiz into the Pacific waters at Long Beach, Rodgers had logged 82 flying hours, and 69 landings.

The aircraft was in terrible shape. In fact, only the vertical rudder and a few struts remained of the original Vin Fiz. The rest was scattered across the American landscape: a wheel here, a wing there, wire everywhere. It had been rebuilt three times.

But, Cal Rodgers philosophized, "That's all part of the game."

Rodgers's crazy game—to publicize a soft drink— helped pave the way for modern transcontinental air travel.

And today, you'd be hard put to find anyone who's ever sipped a "Vin Fiz" . . . or even heard of it.

Starting Time		Finishing Time	
Reading Time		Reading Rate	
Comprehension		Vocabulary	

Comprehension — Read the following questions and statements. For each one, put an *x* in the box before the option that contains the most complete or accurate answer. Check your answers in the Answer Key on page 107.

1. Rodgers came from a family of
   ☐ a. great wealth.
   ☐ b. politicians.
   ☐ c. pilots.
   ☐ d. adventurers.

2. After Rodgers knew he had lost the prize money, his
   ☐ a. ambition fizzled.
   ☐ b. plane was destroyed.
   ☐ c. determination intensified.
   ☐ d. sponsor withdrew.

3. The flight to the Pacific took approximately
   ☐ a. 30 days.
   ☐ b. 40 days.
   ☐ c. 50 days.
   ☐ d. 75 days.

4. Rodgers's accomplishment
   ☐ a. had no lasting value.
   ☐ b. helped shape the future of aviation.
   ☐ c. made him a legend in American history.
   ☐ d. proved that planes had great commercial value.

5. It could be said of Rodgers that he
   ☐ a. flew by the seat of his pants.
   ☐ b. risked the lives of spectators.
   ☐ c. observed the rules of safety.
   ☐ d. relied on electronic equipment.

6. The $50,000 prize offered by William Randolph Hearst most probably
   ☐ a. damaged Hearst's publishing empire.
   ☐ b. advanced the cause of flying.
   ☐ c. alarmed the military establishment.
   ☐ d. attracted no other entry.

7. The Vin Fiz caused a sensation wherever it
   went because
   ☐ a. Rodgers was well liked.
   ☐ b. flying was a popular sport.
   ☐ c. airplanes were expensive.
   ☐ d. flying was a novelty.

8. Rodgers's statements reveal
   ☐ a. an insensitive nature.
   ☐ b. a high level of tension.
   ☐ c. a scornful view of the world.
   ☐ d. a cavalier attitude.

9. The word which best describes Rodgers's
   personality is
   ☐ a. unstable.   ☐ c. greedy.
   ☐ b. predictable.   ☐ d. determined.

10. The opening sentence is an example of
    ☐ a. an understatement.
    ☐ b. an overstatement.
    ☐ c. a metaphor.
    ☐ d. a simile.

Comprehension Skills

1. recalling specific facts	6. making a judgment
2. retaining concepts	7. making an inference
3. organizing facts	8. recognizing tone
4. understanding the main idea	9. understanding characters
5. drawing a conclusion	10. appreciation of literary forms

Study Skills, Part One—Following is a passage with blanks where words have been omitted. Next to the passage are groups of five words, one group for each blank. Complete the passage by selecting the correct word for each of the blanks.

Building Vocabulary

There is a vital connection between language and learning ability and between good grades and the ability to communicate your thoughts clearly and accurately.

An academic curriculum incorporates many subjects, each of which is characterized by its own vocabulary of _(1)_ terms. These terms must be understood if the subject is to be mastered.

All teachers, when evaluating and grading students, _(2)_ those who can express their understanding of key concepts and fundamental facts clearly and concisely. Students display this kind of understanding through their use of _(3)_ terminology. Thus, familiarity with the vocabulary of a subject opens the avenues of communication between student and _(4)_ .

This is not to say that random flaunting of specialized terms will deceive instructors, but it stands to reason that as you acquire the vocabulary of a subject, you will also be accumulating fundamental knowledge in that field. This becomes the base on which new _(5)_ is acquired and assimilated during your regular study.

It is a fact that familiar material is more easily read and understood than _(6)_ material. This explains why we all tend to read articles in our field of interest with ease; we already have the necessary background of information. And this also explains why we sometimes find new subjects dull and uninteresting. Learning the basic vocabulary of a subject gives us a _(7)_ to build on and assures that our study of that field will be profitable.

(1)   successive   borrowed
   general   specialized   correlated

(2)   reward   punish
   appreciate   suspect   notice

(3)   appropriate   random
   useless   helpful   enthusiastic

(4)   peers   friend
   teacher   parent   employer

(5)   words   friends
   associations   learning   principles

(6)   easy   new
   old   difficult   technical

(7)   motivation   orientation
   introduction   foundation   dictation

Study Skills, Part Two—Read the study skills passage again, paying special attention to the lesson being taught. Then, without looking back at the passage, complete each sentence below by writing in the missing word or words. Check the Answer Key on page 107 for the answers to Study Skills, Part One, and Study Skills, Part Two.

1. The specialized vocabulary of a subject must be understood if the subject is to be _____ .

2. Knowledge of vocabulary enables a student to express his _____ of the key concepts of a subject.

3. Acquiring a specific vocabulary also adds to fundamental _____ in a particular field.

4. We read articles about familiar subjects with ease because we already have a _____ of information.

5. Unfamiliar materials often seem dull and _____ .

12 The Standard of Living

by Dorothy Parker

Vocabulary—The five words below are from the story you are about to read. Study the words and their meanings. Then complete the ten sentences that follow, using one of the five words to fill in the blank in each sentence. Mark your answer by writing the letter of the word on the line before the sentence. Check your answers in the Answer Key on page 107.

A. arrogant: proud; haughty

B. lament: grief; sorrow

C. evolved: developed

D. bequest: something passed on or handed down; legacy

E. disdain: scorn; aloofness

_____ 1. Midge and Annabel eyed the jewelry store clerk with _____ .

_____ 2. The game Annabel and Midge played had _____ into an absorbing pastime.

_____ 3. After playing the game with her, Annabel viewed Sylvia with _____ .

_____ 4. In reality, neither Annabel nor Midge was likely to be the recipient of a large _____ .

_____ 5. Annabel accepted the departure of male acquaintances without _____ .

_____ 6. After pricing the pearls, the girls lost their _____ demeanor.

_____ 7. The sum of the _____ had been agreed upon in advance.

_____ 8. _____ over the death of their benefactor was not part of the game.

_____ 9. The two girls carried themselves with an _____ air.

_____ 10. The relationship between Midge and Annabel had _____ into a deep friendship.

Annabel and Midge came out of the tea room with the arrogant slow gait of the leisured, for their Saturday afternoon stretched ahead of them. They had lunched, as was their wont, on sugar, starches, oils, and butterfats. Usually they ate sandwiches of spongy new white bread greased with butter and mayonnaise; they ate thick wedges of cake lying wet beneath ice cream and whipped cream and melted chocolate gritty with nuts. As alternates, they ate patties, sweating beads of inferior oil, containing bits of bland meat bogged in pale, stiffening sauce; they ate pastries, limber under rigid

Slowly the disdain went, slowly and completely, and with it went the regal carriage and tread.

icing, filled with an indeterminate yellow sweet stuff, not still solid, not yet liquid, like salve that has been left in the sun. They chose no other sort of food, nor did they consider it. And their skin was like the petals of wood anemones, and their bellies were as flat and their flanks as lean as those of young Indian braves.

Annabel and Midge had been best friends almost from the day that Midge had found a job as stenographer with the firm that employed Annabel. By now, Annabel, two years longer in the stenographic department, had worked up to the wages of eighteen dollars and fifty cents a week; Midge was still at sixteen dollars. Each girl lived at home with her family and paid half her salary to its support.

The girls sat side by side at their desks, they lunched together every noon, together they set out for home at the end of the day's work. Many of their evenings and most of their Sundays were passed in each other's company. Often they were joined by two young men, but there was no steadiness to any such quartet; the two young men would give place, unlamented, to two other young men, and lament would have been inappropriate, really, since the newcomers were scarcely distinguishable from their predecessors. Invariably the girls spent the fine idle hours of their hot-weather Saturday afternoons together. Constant use had not worn ragged the fabric of their friendship.

They looked alike, though the resemblance did not lie in their features. It was in the shape of their bodies, their movements, their style, and their adornments. Annabel and Midge did, and completely, all that young office workers are besought not to do. They painted their lips and their nails, they darkened their lashes and lightened their hair, and scent seemed to shimmer from them. They wore thin, bright dresses, tight over their breasts and high on their legs, and tilted slippers, fancifully strapped. They looked conspicuous and cheap and charming.

Now, as they walked across to Fifth Avenue with their skirts swirled by the hot wind, they received audible admiration. Young men grouped lethargically about newsstands awarded them murmurs, exclamations, even—the ultimate tribute—whistles. Annabel and Midge passed without the condescension of hurrying their pace; they held their heads higher and set their feet with exquisite precision, as if they stepped over the necks of peasants.

Always the girls went to walk on Fifth Avenue on their free afternoons, for it was the ideal ground for their favorite game. The game could be played anywhere, and indeed, was, but the great shop windows stimulated the two players to their best form.

Annabel had invented the game; or rather she had evolved it from an old one. Basically, it was no more than the ancient sport of what-would-you-do-if-you-had-a-million-dollars? But Annabel had drawn a new set of rules for it, had narrowed it, pointed it, made it stricter. Like all games, it was the more absorbing for being more difficult.

Annabel's version went like this: You must suppose that somebody dies and leaves you a million dollars, cool. But there is a condition to the bequest. It is stated in the will that you must spend every nickel of the money on yourself.

There lay the hazard of the game. If, when playing it, you forgot and listed among your expenditures the rental of a new apartment for your family, for example, you lost your turn to the other player. It was astonishing how many—and some of them among the experts, too—would forfeit all their innings by such slips.

It was essential, of course, that it be played in passionate seriousness. Each purchase must be carefully considered and, if necessary, supported by argument. There was no zest to playing it wildly. Once Annabel had introduced the game to Sylvia, another girl who worked in the office. She explained the rules to Sylvia and then offered her the gambit "What would be the first thing you'd do?" Sylvia had not shown the decency of even a second of hesitation. "Well," she said, "the first thing I'd do, I'd go out and hire somebody to shoot Mrs. Gary Cooper, and then . . ." So it is to be seen that she was no fun.

But Annabel and Midge were surely born to be comrades, for Midge played the game like a master from the moment she learned it. It was she who added the touches that made the whole thing cozier. According to Midge's innovations, the eccentric who died and left you the money was not anybody you loved, or, for the matter of that, anybody you even knew. It was somebody who had seen you somewhere and had thought, "That girl ought to have lots of nice things. I'm going to leave her a million dollars when I die." And the death was to be neither untimely nor painful. Your benefactor, full of years and comfortably ready to depart, was to slip softly away during sleep and go right to heaven. These embroideries permitted Annabel and Midge to play their game in the luxury of peaceful consciences.

Midge played with a seriousness that was not only proper but extreme. The single strain on the girls' friendship had followed an announcement once made by Annabel that the first thing she would buy with her million dollars would be a silver-fox coat. It was as if she had struck Midge across the mouth. When Midge recovered her breath, she cried that she couldn't imagine how Annabel could do such a thing—silver-fox coats were so common! Annabel defended her taste with the retort that they were not common, either. Midge then said that they were so. She added that everybody had a silver-fox coat. She went on, with perhaps a slight loss of head, to declare that she herself wouldn't be caught dead in silver fox.

For the next few days, though the girls saw each other as constantly, their conversation was careful and infrequent, and they did not once play their game. Then one morning, as soon as Annabel entered the office, she came to Midge and said she had changed her mind. She would not buy a silver-fox coat with any part of her million dollars. Immediately on receiving the legacy, she would select a coat of mink.

Midge smiled and her eyes shone. "I think," she said, "you're doing absolutely the right thing."

Now, as they walked along Fifth Avenue, they played the game anew. It was one of those days with which September is repeatedly cursed; hot and glaring, with slivers of dust in the wind. People drooped and shambled, but the girls carried themselves tall and walked a straight line, as befitted young heiresses on their afternoon promenade. There was no longer need for them to start the game at its formal opening. Annabel went direct to the heart of it.

"All right," she said. "So you've got this million dollars. So what would be the first thing you'd do?"

"Well, the first thing I'd do," Midge said, "I'd get a mink coat." But she said it mechanically, as if she were giving the memorized answer to an expected question.

"Yes," Annabel said. "I think you ought to. The terribly dark kind of mink." But she, too, spoke as if by rote. It was too hot; fur, no matter how dark and sleek and supple, was horrid to the thoughts.

They stepped along in silence for a while. Then Midge's eye was caught by a shop window. Cool, lovely gleamings were there set off by chaste and elegant darkness.

"No," Midge said. "I take it back. I wouldn't get a mink coat the first thing. Know what I'd do? I'd get a string of pearls. Real pearls."

Annabel's eyes turned to follow Midge's.

"Yes," she said, slowly. "I think that's a kind of a good idea. And it would make sense, too. Because you can wear pearls with anything."

Together they went over to the shop window and stood pressed against it. It contained but one object—a double row of great, even pearls clasped by a deep emerald around a little pink velvet throat.

"What do you suppose they cost?" Annabel said.

"Gee, I don't know," Midge said. "Plenty, I guess."

"Like a thousand dollars?" Annabel said.

"Oh, I guess like more," Midge said. "On account of the emerald."

"Well, like ten thousand dollars?" Annabel said.

"Gee, I wouldn't even know," Midge said.

The devil nudged Annabel in the ribs. "Dare you to go in and price them," she said.

"Like fun!" Midge said.

"Dare you," Annabel said.

"Why, a store like this couldn't even be open this afternoon," Midge said.

"Yes, it is so, too," Annabel said. "People just came out. And there's a doorman on. Dare you."

"Well," Midge said. "But you've got to come too."

They tendered thanks, icily, to the doorman for ushering them into the shop. It was cool and quiet, a broad, gracious room with paneled walls and soft carpet. But the girls wore expressions of bitter disdain, as if they stood in a sty.

A slim, immaculate clerk came to them and bowed. His neat face showed no astonishment at their appearance.

"Good afternoon," he said. He implied that he would never forget it if they would grant him the favor of accepting his soft-spoken greeting.

"Good afternoon," Annabel and Midge said together, and in like freezing accents.

"Is there something—?" the clerk said.

"Oh, we're just looking," Annabel said. It was as if she flung the words down from a dais.

The clerk bowed.

"My friend and myself merely happened to be passing," Midge said, and stopped, seeming to listen to the phrase. "My friend here and myself," she went on, "merely happened to be wondering how much are those pearls you've got in your window?"

"Ah, yes," the clerk said. "The double rope. That is two hundred and fifty thousand dollars, Madam."

"I see," Midge said.

The clerk bowed. "An exceptionally beautiful necklace," he said. "Would you care to look at it?"

"No, thank you," Annabel said.

"My friend and myself merely happened to be passing," Midge said.

They turned to go; to go, from their manner, where the tumbrel awaited them. The clerk sprang ahead and opened the door. He bowed as they swept by him.

The girls went on along the Avenue and disdain was still on their faces.

"Honestly!" Annabel said. "Can you imagine a thing like that?"

"Two hundred and fifty thousand dollars!" Midge said. "That's a quarter of a million dollars right there!"

"He's got his nerve!" Annabel said.

They walked on. Slowly the disdain went, slowly and completely as if drained from them, and with it went the regal carriage and tread. Their shoulders drooped and they dragged their feet; they bumped against each other, without notice or apology, and caromed away again. They were silent and their eyes were cloudy.

Suddenly Midge straightened her back, flung her head high, and spoke, clear and strong.

"Listen, Annabel," she said. "Look. Suppose there was this terribly rich person, see? You don't know this person, but this person has seen you somewhere and wants to do something for you. Well, it's a terribly old person, see? And so this person dies, just like going to sleep, and leaves you ten million dollars. Now, what would be the first thing you'd do?"

Her literary criticism and witty conversation won American poet and short story writer Dorothy Parker fame. Most of her verse and stories express a humorous but cynical disappointment with life. She often wrote in a biting, ironic style about the loss of love and idealism. Parker was born in West End, New Jersey, in 1893 and lived in New York City for most of her life. She contributed regularly to *The New Yorker* and the magazine's book review column for several years, and belonged to the Algonquin Round Table in the 1920s—a group of famous writers who met regularly at the Algonquin Hotel in New York City.

Starting Time		Finishing Time	
Reading Time		Reading Rate	
Comprehension		Vocabulary	

Comprehension— Read the following questions and statements. For each one, put an *x* in the box before the option that contains the most complete or accurate answer. Check your answers in the Answer Key on page 107.

1. The game had been perfected by
   □ a. Annabel.
   □ b. Midge.
   □ c. Sylvia.
   □ d. Dorothy.

2. The kinds of food the girls ate for lunch
   □ a. represent a well-balanced diet.
   □ b. are bought by the wealthy.
   □ c. did not cost much.
   □ d. did not affect their weight.

3. Midge agreed to ask the price of the pearls only after Annabel promised
   □ a. not to laugh.
   □ b. to go into the store with her.
   □ c. never to tell anyone.
   □ d. to let Sylvia join the game.

4. The selection deals with
   □ a. the unhappy lot of secretaries.
   □ b. the unequal distribution of wealth.
   □ c. an irregularity in human behavior.
   □ d. an understandable human tendency.

5. The girls lived
   □ a. glamorous lives.
   □ b. conventional lives.
   □ c. mysterious lives.
   □ d. protected lives.

6. The game played by Annabel and Midge was a
   □ a. form of escapism.
   □ b. dangerous deception.
   □ c. common pastime.
   □ d. stimulus to ambition.

7. Evidence in the story suggests that Annabel and Midge were
   □ a. looking for another job.
   □ b. expecting a large inheritance.
   □ c. interested in matrimony.
   □ d. unhappy with their condition.

8. The opening paragraph suggests an atmosphere of
   □ a. indulgent idleness.
   □ b. helpless confusion.
   □ c. emotional tenseness.
   □ d. vague suspicion.

9. Annabel and Midge were
   □ a. sophisticated.
   □ b. deceitful.
   □ c. immature.
   □ d. inconsiderate.

10. The sentence, "Constant use had not worn ragged the fabric of their friendship," means that the girls
    □ a. did not tire of each other's company.
    □ b. preferred the company of male friends.
    □ c. were ashamed of their clothes.
    □ d. tolerated each other with difficulty.

Comprehension Skills

1. recalling specific facts	6. making a judgment
2. retaining concepts	7. making an inference
3. organizing facts	8. recognizing tone
4. understanding the main idea	9. understanding characters
5. drawing a conclusion	10. appreciation of literary forms

Study Skills, Part One—Following is a passage with blanks where words have been omitted. Next to the passage are groups of five words, one group for each blank. Complete the passage by selecting the correct word for each of the blanks.

Specialized Word Lists, I

The two prime sources of words for your specialized lists are your instructors and your textbooks.

Listen during class lectures for the words the speaker repeats and ___(1)___ . These are likely candidates. Identifying key words will present no problem because experienced lecturers understand the limitations of their listeners. They know that major ___(2)___ need the emphasis of repeated exposure. What would be in bold print in a textbook must be conveyed to students verbally. Be alert for unusual inflection and ___(3)___ which may be given to certain words. These are considered important by the lecturer. Especially important terms are often written on the blackboard.

Listen to questions asked by the speaker. Oral ___(4)___ is often used to draw greater attention to important points under discussion.

Another clue to identifying important words and ideas may be found in the length of time devoted to discussion of a single topic. Important points deserve ___(5)___ time.

When you discover that a major term is being presented, try to record the ___(6)___ definition or explanation given. Being a specialist, your instructor will use precise terminology when defining a concept. Be sure to capture new words exactly as they are used. Indicate with an asterisk or star in your notes that here is a word for your ___(7)___ list.

[1]	rotates	emphasizes
	discards	ignores	shouts

(2)	points	errors
	expectations	illustrations	performers

(3)	appreciation	pressure
	concealment	strain	stress

(4)	humor	quizzing
	statement	concept	explanation

(5)	more	special
	primary	less	standard

(6)	first	only
	supplementary	general	exact

(7)	shopping	general
	specialized	surplus	discard

Study Skills, Part Two—Read the study skills passage again, paying special attention to the lesson being taught. Then, without looking back at the passage, complete each sentence below by writing in the missing word or words. Check the Answer Key on page 107 for the answers to Study Skills, Part One, and Study Skills, Part Two.

1. Two prime sources for specialized vocabulary lists are your _____ and your textbooks.

2. Experienced instructors make it easy to _____ key words.

3. Important words are emphasized, _____ , and often written on the board.

4. The instructor also uses oral _____ to draw attention to important points.

5. Because he is a specialist, the instructor will use _____ terminology when defining a concept.

13 | Letter from France

by Maya Angelou

Vocabulary—The five words below are from the story you are about to read. Study the words and their meanings. Then complete the ten sentences that follow, using one of the five words to fill in the blank in each sentence. Mark your answer by writing the letter of the word on the line before the sentence. Check your answers in the Answer Key on page 107.

A. propensity: tendency

B. merited: deserved

C. intrepid: fearless

D. chagrin: embarrassment

E. cajoled: coaxed; wheedled

_____ 1. The author _____ a friend into letting her use a Victorian house in South London.

_____ 2. The author had a _____ to compare new surroundings to Berkeley.

_____ 3. After the long drive, the author felt she _____ a good night's sleep.

_____ 4. Much to his _____ , Paul missed his chance to see Rouen.

_____ 5. The author admires people who are _____ adventurers.

_____ 6. James Baldwin showed no _____ when the author announced she would be leaving in the morning.

_____ 7. The author believed that hard work _____ a reward.

_____ 8. Some people have a _____ to travel.

_____ 9. The author easily _____ Paul into taking a European vacation.

_____ 10. Paul had a reputation for being an _____ traveler.

I have seen cotton pickers in Arkansas, longshoremen on San Francisco's waterfront, camel drivers in Egypt, cocoa merchants in Ghana, taxi drivers in New York, and winegrowers in France. What I've learned from watching the exertions of these varied people is that they work nearly as diligently as writers.

Obviously, it was time to move on to more exotic places.

Daily Mail livened my morning tea, but the *San Francisco Chronicle* did the same for my coffee.

Obviously, it was time to move on to more exotic places.

James Baldwin had invited me many times to come and see his house in the south of France. He has long been my friend, brother,

Forget the old romantic myth that would cast writers as "artistes" who inhale only rarefied air and sip from nectar-filled cups held by generous Muses. Writing is work. Or so I reckon it.

From the window of my cottage in the Berkeley Hills, I watched the sun glinting on the windshields of cars crossing the Golden Gate Bridge and the traffic helicopter hovering like a metal dragonfly over the silver Bay Bridge. Everybody was going someplace. Since I had just turned in my latest book to my editor, I didn't think anyone deserved a trip more than I.

During this time, I had a houseguest (I'll call him Paul Du Feu) who was a world traveler. We had spent many nights in front of my fireplace laughing together at his experiences in Canadian forests, or in living rough on the beaches of Spain, or selling cars in Germany. He dared adventure and always landed on his feet. Admitting my own lack of daring and my propensity to stay on the beaten path, I thought he would make the ideal traveling companion. He agreed. And since he had just turned in a finished manuscript, he said he, too, merited a vacation.

The TWA Red Eye Special (leaving San Francisco at 10:00 P.M. and arriving New York at 6:00 A.M.) was just what I expected it to be. Although the service was first class, the jet lag and cocktails at 37,000 feet made me a perfect "before" model for an eyewash advertisement. New York City at dawn is as nice as it's likely to be, so from the air I watched the skyscrapers through rose-colored eyes and projected myself toward the evening transatlantic flight.

The next morning, from London's Heathrow Airport (where all but tourists respect the taxi queues), we traveled to South London where friends had lent us a newly renovated Victorian house. The bay windows looked out over Wandsworth Common, and the backyard reminded me of the garden I left in California. Mornings I slept late, then worked desultorily among the string beans while Paul raked casually around the tomatoes. At noon, we walked to the corner pub and drank our share of good lukewarm beer, appropriately called "bitter."

After a few weeks, I had to admit that my life had not qualitatively changed. I had simply changed locale. True, London's streets were clean and colorful, but so are Berkeley's. Admittedly, shop attendants and waitresses were courteous, but then so are they in the Bay Area. The

and favorite writer. Since I was so near, since London was reminding me more and more of northern California, since Paul was beginning to show just an edge of edginess, I suggested that we tear ourselves loose and bound over to southern France. He agreed readily.

We packed the hardly used gardening tools, put the borrowed house in order, and telphoned BEA for reservations to Nice. When we were told the ticket rates (seventy-eight pounds sterling each, one way, London-Nice) we were nearly shocked into remaining in London. But Paul, the intrepid adventurer, suggested buying a car, an old used car, preferably a retired post-office van ("one driver, whose use of it was mostly in parking along shady streets"). Fortunately, a friend had an Austin Mini Countryman he needed to rid himself of. The car was in "excellent condition," only nine years old, and had spent most of those years "parked along shady streets."

We drove aboard the British Sea Link Ferry in New Haven at 10:00 P.M., and at midnight, as the ship pulled out into the channel, we toasted each other in the well-appointed dining room with a solid French wine that was nearly as good as Gallo's Hearty Burgundy.

Dawn in Dieppe. Three times the morning fog lifted for two seconds as I picked the car's way through the town's narrow cobbled streets and out onto a gray highway. An arrow promised Rouen and, since Paul was sleeping off our shipboard celebration, I had no choice but to trust the promise. A pale sun rose on the Normandy countryside, and it was a dreary setting for an Ingmar Bergman film. But as the light strengthened, the fertility of the land was more evident. Thatched cottages and prosperous farmhouses sat back from the highway in San Joaquin Valley green. I tried to people the landscape with conquering Normans from old history books or allied troops from World War II, but the tiny car wrestled along the road like a hooked trout, and before I could let my attention wander, I had driven through Rouen and reached the outskirts of a fairly large town.

Paul awoke, ashamed that he had slept through the hard part of the drive. I did nothing to dispel his chagrin except to quote Thomas Wolfe on man:

> He lived and he was here! He needed speech to ask
> for bread and he had Christ! He needed songs to sing
> in battle and he had Homer! He wove the robes of

Solomon! He needed a temple to propitiate his God and he made Chartres!

"Are we in Chartres?"

"*Oui.*"

We sat at a sidewalk restaurant off a cobbled square and had our first *petit pain* and *café au lait*. The wonders of fresh bread, sweet butter, and hot coffee were partly lost on me since I was still trying to unfold my six-foot frame from the pattern the small car was molding me into. Paul popped under the wheel and guided the car back to the highway. Over the rooftops I spied the spires of the cathedral called by Rodin the "Acropolis of France." Once back on the road, I mentally ticked off Chartres. It has been done.

We hurtled, devil-may-care, through rural France at the car's top speed of 50 mph. By one o'clock, we stormed into Bourges. The Gothic 15th-Century town didn't warm under the bright sunlight, and visions of medieval barbarity sugarplummed in my head. Since we carried no *Guide Michelin* or gourmet's map, we chose the first restaurant we saw and had a fine meal. The menu and the name of the establishment are forgotten, but the local Sancerre wine left an indelible and good memory.

My dashing companion jangled the car keys and said no to another bottle of the local vintage. Over the steep roofs, I think I caught sight of a corner of the famous Bourges cathedral. As we tootled to the highway, I checked off Bourges. It was done.

The meadows and pastures unfolded slowly out the Austin's sliding windows in nearly the same rhythm that my legs, shoulders, and arms were atrophying within the car. By five-thirty we drove into Roanne, and I thought it would be easier to sleep where I was than to demand the improbable of my aching body.

We moved into the fading but elegant Hotel Centrale as if we planned to stay for a month. Paul and a too-thin bellboy carried our six large bags and a box of books into the hotel's strong room, since one of the car doors refused to lock securely. A long steamy bath cajoled my muscles into resuming their work, and by nine o'clock we followed the hotel manager's directions to the Restaurant Alsace-Lorraine. We ate a well-prepared and abundantly served dinner and walked the quiet dark streets back to the hotel.

Morning found us pleated back into the car and on the highway. Lyons flew by in a haze of pink hill chateaux and modern high-rise buildings.

We drove, finally, to Cannes and up the twisting roads to St. Paul. Near midnight we parked our pressure cooker at the edge of a tiny square and saw men in short sleeves playing *boule* under the lights. The elegant Colombe d'Or restaurant, where Picasso, Yves Montand, Simone Signoret, and Baldwin were known to "lift a few," faced the square. We ordered drinks at a lesser known bistro nearby and telephoned Jimmy. In minutes he strode into the square, jacket flung casually across his shoulders, a wide grin across his face. He is a celebrity. Tourists and natives alike recognized him, and he returned their salutes warmly— then gave me a family embrace. He said he'd guide us to his house.

The villa suits a great writer and especially James Baldwin. It is glamorous. Baldwin is glamorous. It is romantic. The romance of Baldwin lies in the fact that his warmth makes us nearly forget that he is a giant. And the house is comfortable to be near.

Yet, with the exception of a gay reunion with my friend, the destination was to prove anticlimactic. My soreness resisted the solace of a bed. The smells of old bread, melting butter, and stale wine from the car, clung to the lining of my nostrils and made it difficult for me to appreciate the talents of Baldwin's highly praised cook.

We sat under a grapevine-laced arbor that has its counterpart on a ranch in Sonoma owned by a winegrowing friend. The company's conversation dealt with Life, Taxes, Politics, Love, and the Arts. The same subjects we had all discussed in Paris, London, New York, and Berkeley.

Outside the walled villa, the streets of St. Paul, LaColle, Cagnes, and Cannes resembled Macy's toy department during the Christmas season. Cars crawled 5 mph along the undoubtedly beautiful corniche, and pedestrians more anxious for their tans than in staying whole, wedged between bumpers on their way to the sea. It was a sunny Sunday afternoon in Sausalito, which had been leased to beauty-hungry tourists from Los Angeles.

"How long do you want to stay?"

I hoped I was reading Paul correctly. "I'm ready to head north," I answered.

He smiled. "We'll leave at dawn."

That suited me.

I said good-bye to my friends in St. Paul and spent the next day and the next waving fond adieus to the familiar lay-bys. A day later, I was gathering fresh zucchini, eggplant, and onions from my backyard in Berkeley. I made a *ratatouille provencale.*

Aside from being a well-known writer, Maya Angelou has worked as an actress, film director, lecturer, and musician. During the 1960s, she worked as an editor and reporter in Africa, becoming the first woman editor of an English-language magazine. She published several novels in the 1970s and wrote the screenplay and musical score for the film *Georgia, Georgia* in 1972. In 1975 she received the *Ladies Home Journal* "Woman of the Year Award" for Communications. Other honors include a Tony nomination for best supporting actress for her performance in the 1977 television series *Roots,* numerous honorary degrees, and a place in the Black Filmmakers Hall of Fame.

Maya Angelou is currently a member of Actor's Equity, the Director's Guild of America, and the advisory board of the Women's Prison Association.

Starting Time		Finishing Time	
Reading Time		Reading Rate	
Comprehension		Vocabulary	

Comprehension — Read the following questions and statements. For each one, put an *x* in the box before the option that contains the most complete or accurate answer. Check your answers in the Answer Key on page 107.

1. The author found the Austin car
   - ☐ a. unbearable.
   - ☐ b. uncomfortable.
   - ☐ c. unpredictable.
   - ☐ d. unmanageable.

2. The hardest working people, from the author's point of view, are
   - ☐ a. cotton pickers.
   - ☐ b. taxi drivers.
   - ☐ c. writers.
   - ☐ d. longshoremen.

3. The author stayed in South London for
   - ☐ a. one night.
   - ☐ b. three nights.
   - ☐ c. several weeks.
   - ☐ d. six months.

4. The author gradually came to realize that
   - ☐ a. there is high adventure on the open road.
   - ☐ b. writers are very special people.
   - ☐ c. Europeans are very sophisticated.
   - ☐ d. there is no place like home.

5. The author's favorite habitat is
   - ☐ a. South London.
   - ☐ b. Berkeley, California.
   - ☐ c. Rouen, France.
   - ☐ d. New York City.

6. The author's decision to go on vacation seems
   - ☐ a. impractical.
   - ☐ b. comical.
   - ☐ c. sound.
   - ☐ d. rash.

7. The TWA Red Eye Special
   - ☐ a. offers second-rate service.
   - ☐ b. is an unpopular flight.
   - ☐ c. is never on time.
   - ☐ d. seems appropriately named.

8. The author's mood during her travels abroad seems
   - ☐ a. restless.
   - ☐ b. confused.
   - ☐ c. content.
   - ☐ d. bitter.

9. The author considers herself
   - ☐ a. a daring traveler.
   - ☐ b. a typical nonconformist.
   - ☐ c. a conservative person.
   - ☐ d. an incurable romantic.

10. The author has a talent for
   - ☐ a. creating suspense.
   - ☐ b. biting satire.
   - ☐ c. figurative language.
   - ☐ d. informational writing.

Comprehension Skills

1. recalling specific facts	6. making a judgment
2. retaining concepts	7. making an inference
3. organizing facts	8. recognizing tone
4. understanding the main idea	9. understanding characters
5. drawing a conclusion	10. appreciation of literary forms

Study Skills, Part One — Following is a passage with blanks where words have been omitted. Next to the passage are groups of five words, one group for each blank. Complete the passage by selecting the correct word for each of the blanks.

Specialized Word Lists, II

Another source of specialized terms is your textbook. Alert readers soon discover that a ___(1)___ frequently hinges on only five or six major concepts. Often there are key words associated with these concepts; these are the words to collect and learn.

Such words are often highlighted in bold print or ___(2)___ . If you need additional assurance, refer to questions or other types of summaries that frequently appear at the end of the chapter. These summaries will emphasize major points, the ones the writer wants you to understand and remember.

When you have ___(3)___ the important terms for the unit you are studying, write them down with accompanying

(1)
book	chapter	
paragraph	sentence	phrase

(2)
commas	chapters	
headings	periods	sentences

(3)
located	finished	
repelled	created	lost

definitions and explanations. As you read through the chapter, try to understand these new words and the concepts they represent as fully as you can. If you are not satisfied that your understanding is complete ___(4)___ your first reading, it may be necessary to reread parts of the chapter.

Frequently, these same words will be the ones that are emphasized in ___(5)___ . When this is the case, the instructor will often explain the new terms in words different from those in the text. Be alert to catch these variances because they ___(6)___ the meaning of an idea, often increasing its significance for you and making it easier to understand.

A ___(7)___ aspect of having studied and learned a term *before* class is that the speaker's remarks now make more sense to you. You will also find that your mind will wander less because of the greater interest and understanding that advanced knowledge fosters.

| (4) | | preceding | | renewing |
| | during | | repeating | following |

| (5) | | textbooks | | class |
| | movies | | illustrations | studies |

| (6) | | enrich | | contradict |
| | specify | | define | change |

| (7) | | miniature | | repeated |
| | minus | | bonus | friendly |

Study Skills, Part Two—Read the study skills passage again, paying special attention to the lesson being taught. Then, without looking back at the passage, complete each sentence below by writing in the missing word or words. Check the Answer Key on page 107 for the answers to Study Skills, Part One, and Study Skills, Part Two.

1. Key words associated with _____ points are the words to learn.

2. Questions and other types of _____ at the end of the

   chapter emphasize important points.

3. Write down important terms with accompanying _____

   and explanations.

4. Instructors often add to the meaning of a word defined in the text and thereby

   _____ its significance.

5. Advance knowledge often produces greater _____ in and

   understanding of a subject.

14 | # Velcro: The Final Frontier

by Judith Stone

Vocabulary—The five words below are from the story you are about to read. Study the words and their meanings. Then complete the ten sentences that follow, using one of the five words to fill in the blank in each sentence. Mark your answer by writing the letter of the word on the line before the sentence. Check your answers in the Answer Key on page 108.

A. component: element; part

B. undaunted: not discouraged

C. expired: ended; ran out

D. vouch: verify; speak on behalf of

E. innovative: new; original

_____ 1. The members of the band ZZ Top can _____ for Velcro USA's concern over the generic use of the word "velcro."

_____ 2. Velcro's basic patent _____ in 1978.

_____ 3. Hundreds of _____ uses have been found for Velcro.

_____ 4. Manny Cardinale, vice president of sales, can _____ for the fact that Velcro USA takes itself seriously.

_____ 5. Kenner Parker Toys found an _____ use for Velcro with its Special Blessings dolls.

_____ 6. David Letterman was apparently _____ by the prospect of sticking himself to a wall with Velcro.

_____ 7. One _____ of Velcro is a strip of nylon hooks.

_____ 8. Velcro has become a _____ in many shoes.

_____ 9. Velcro's usefulness has certainly not _____ .

_____ 10. Competing companies seem _____ by the domination of Velcro USA in the hook-and-loop industry.

Fashion designer Jimmy Z has pronounced it the mating call of the eighties: the *rrrrip!* of Velcro pieces being peeled apart. The no-fumble fastener has replaced zipper, button, snap, and hook on enough of America's clothing to make its distinctive strip a stirring sound of seduction—the signal that something's going on because something's coming off.

But suppose you're making war, not love. Today's Army has busted its buttons and promoted Velcro to ranking uniform pocket closure. Yet in combat that telltale rip could mean R.I.P. if the noise were to reveal a soldier's position. That's why the Army asked for silent Velcro.

Can you really use Velcro to secure an airplane wing? Or perfect an artificial heart? Or stick David Letterman to a wall?

"We have, in fact, figured out the source of the noise and informed the Army," says William Kennedy, vice president of technology for Velcro Group, part of the firm that makes the original hook-and-loop fastener. The stuff is woven, usually of nylon, in such a way that thousands of tiny hooks on one side engage thousands of tiny loops on the other. "We've reduced the noise level by over ninety-five percent," says Kennedy. He adds that the mechanics of the new product are hush-hush: "I'd rather not talk about it at this stage of the game. Our patent applications are filed but they aren't issued yet." But you can know this: the racket is 60 percent the hook's fault and 40 percent the loop's.

The saga of stealth Velcro wasn't the only gripping story to emerge from a visit to the Manchester, New Hampshire, headquarters of Velcro USA. "We're wrongly perceived by many as a gimmick fastener," says Manny Cardinale, vice president of sales. "Velcro is fun, but it's a serious product."

Could a gimmick fastener hold together a Pontiac 6000? Could a gimmick fastener keep an airplane wing intact? Could it stick David Letterman to a wall? What was the Jarvik-7 artificial heart, chopped liver? That device's two pumping chambers were secured with Velcro so that if only one malfunctioned, as it did in pioneer patient Barney Clark, doctors could pop it out and replace it without having to remove the other one. "And the shuttle couldn't have flown without us," Kennedy says.

You get the feeling that the 600 employees here at headquarters think of the space program as a spin-off of Velcro research. "There were ten thousand square inches of tape on each shuttle," adds Leon Kuiawa, market manager of Velcro's government services division. "Many things in the interior—the food packets, even the astronauts at times—were held down with Astro Velcro, made with Teflon loops, polyester hooks, and a beta glass backing." And a small patch inside their helmets allowed the astronauts to scratch their noses.

The word *Velcro* is mentioned, Kennedy points out, as a component in over 5,000 U.S. patents. The company can't,

of course, control how others use the product, but it likes to keep track. It's also haunted by kleenexphobia: dread of going generic. Velcro's basic patent ran out in 1978; that's meant competition at home and especially in the Far East. Richard Kuhl, Velcro vice president of operations, estimates that there are at least two or three dozen hook-and-loop manufacturers in Taiwan alone.

Velcro USA, a wholly owned subsidiary of a Dutch-registered company with holdings in Europe, Asia, and New Zealand, still leads the market, but its name is a sticky subject. You can call the stuff touch fastener, hook and loop, burr tape, or magic tape, but don't call it Velcro unless you capitalize. A few years ago Velcro USA became ruffled when the hairy metal rock band ZZ Top released a song and video called "Velcro Fly" (which sounded not only generic but unwholesome). The company insisted that the album cover clearly indicate that Velcro is a registered trademark.

Velcro's a womb-to-tomb kind of fastener, used to strap on fetal monitors and seal body bags. Applications range from the sacred (securing the praying hands of Special Blessings, a new doll from Kenner Parker Toys) to the profane (closing Cathy's Cuffs, an accessory for those who put stock in bondage). The medical profession would be strapped without hook and loop. (What did they use to close blood pressure cuffs before Velcro? Nails?) The product turns up in such unexpected places as the M1A1 tank, where it works like a chain and sprocket to help turn the machine gun turret, and in nuclear power plants, where a version of the product woven from stainless steel and Nomex, a flame retardant polymer, holds insulation blankets around radioactive pipes.

Velcro has captured the public's imagination. "We have tremendous customer goodwill," says Kuhl, "although sometimes people accuse us of keeping kids from learning how to tie their shoes." Every week he receives a pile of suggestions for putting hook and loop to work. "Most have already been done, like key rings, pen holders, picture hangers, or wallets," he says, pointing to a thick file of current correspondence next to his Velcro-fastened briefcase. Some include detailed plans; others are hand-scrawled in the heat of inspiration. Most, like the removable designer-jean labels, wouldn't be cost-effective. Or there's some glitch, as with the Velcro-soled slippers that kept the elderly from slipping on slick floors but stuck to carpets. The only unsolicited proposal the company has pursued, Kuhl says, was adding a hook-and-loop-closed pocket to beach towels. But no towel company was interested.

Carter Zelenik, a research associate at the Center for Research in Medical Education and Health Care at Jefferson Medical College in Philadelphia, is undaunted by the company's lack of interest in his globe jigsaw puzzle, on which countries and continents are affixed with Velcro. He'll keep fiddling. "I like the stuff," he says. "I like its natural history. I like the idea that someone got stuck with thistles and learned from it."

The guy who got stuck with thistles was Georges deMestral, a Swiss engineer. One day in 1948 he returned from a walk in the woods, musing over the workings of cockleburs that stuck to his socks and his dog. Examining the burrs under a microscope, he discovered that they were composed of hundreds of tiny hooks that latched on to anything even slightly loopy. He figured out a way to duplicate the hook-and-loop configuration in woven nylon and called the odd product Velcro, for *velvet* and *crochet*, French for hook. Among deMestral's inventions was a Velcro asparagus peeler.

Although the original patent has expired, many parts of the production process are still proprietary. And one nonwoven form of Velcro, a molded plastic hook and loop used in automobile seats, remains under patent. Twenty-four hours a day, five days a week, on clattering high-speed looms, workers weave nylon filament into a loopy fabric that's then dipped in secret sauce. On half of the fabric the loops are snipped to form hooks. "Then the loops are napped to disorient them—a fuzzy surface engages better," Kuhl explains. (Velcro's loops are more confused than anyone else's, which, it seems, makes it a superior product. Velcro shoe fasteners, for example, can cycle—open and close, to us lay people—10,000 times. Kuhl can't vouch for his competitors.) The material is heated to set the nylon's shape memory, dyed, backed, and cut.

Velcro is stronger than people think. Standard Velcro has a shear strength (forced applied to parallel pieces pulled in opposing directions) of about 10 to 15 pounds per square inch. "If I use two hundred square inches," says Kennedy, "I've got a ton of force. The reason that the Letterman thing works is that he's got a lot of area."

The host of *Late Night* performed television's most famous—and perhaps only—Velcro stunt two years ago when he donned coveralls made of hook and made a trampoline-assisted jump onto a wall covered with loop. Last February he reprised the leap for his sixth-anniversary show. Costume designer Susan Hum used 55 yards of two-inch-wide Velcro for his bright red coveralls. The yellow loop wall couldn't be padded, or Letterman wouldn't have hit it with enough force to stick. "David says it kind of hurts," Hum reports.

But it holds. "Some Velcro products have one hundred pounds of shear force per square inch," says Kennedy. "Then all I need is twenty square inches to get a ton of holding power." Recently a team of GM and Velcro engineers experimented with using hook and loop in as many ways as possible on a Pontiac 6000—on seats and ceilings, to hold down the battery and fuel lines, to secure the spare tire. It was also tested as a backup attaching device on a front fender. "After the car had been test-driven the equivalent of fifty thousand miles, the fender was checked," says Kuhl.

"We found that the screws that were supposed to hold it on had either never been put in or had fallen out. But the fender had budged only a couple of millimeters. Unlike a screw, a hook and loop increases in strength when it's vibrated."

Now the company is negotiating with one of the automotive big three to put together a car with Velcro. "And if you can put together a car, why not an airplane?" asks Kennedy. Members of his 34-person R and D team are working on using Velcro in wing fairings, the one-ton sheets of metal molding that smooth the fuselage to the wing. Usually they're held in place with 14,000 titanium rivets; the idea is to replace some of those with hook and loop.

What else does the future hold? In the applications laboratory, where the sales staff help customers find innovative uses for hook and loop—"We tell you where to stick it," says assistant Jackie Puglisi—they're working on a project for Uncle Sam: a Velcro-fastened mailbag easier to schlep than one closed with metal-covered strings. And for Leon Kuiawa, the key word is plastics: "In five to ten years we'll make an impact in cars like the Corvette, which is made of a plastic composite. Drill a hole for a nut and bolt and you interfere with its internal strength. Bond our product into the structure and you can assemble the car."

Kennedy and his staff are working on a longer-lived version of Astro Velcro and on low cost, disposable Velcro for packaging. The R and D people are most interested in custom-engineering performance characteristics. "Suppose we wanted some sort of fail-safe device," says Kennedy, "something that releases after a certain amount of pressure is applied, like a safety valve. We'd like to engineer the product to release at certain forces. The uses of Velcro are almost unlimited."

It's hard not to be inspired. What frontier is left? Edible Velcro comes to mind. If a material can be spun into a filament, says Kennedy, it can be woven into Velcro: "If there becomes a need for edible Velcro, we'll work on it." If? When was the last time he tried to wrap one of those flimsy pancakes around a pile of mooshoo pork? Don't mooshoo shoot and burrito squirt merit as much attention as loose sneakers?

Not every application has taken hold. The Worm Collar, a cylindrical strip of the loop portion of Velcro that slipped around live bait, the better to snag the teeth of striking bass, seemed like a good idea. But not enough customers bit. Wade Fox, Jr., manager of new business development, heard about some kindergartners who played the "Star-Spangled Banner" by opening and closing their Velcro-fastened sneakers, but the product hasn't caught on as a musical instrument. And the strap-on prosthetic device for impotent men was a flop.

Starting Time		Finishing Time	
Reading Time		Reading Rate	
Comprehension		Vocabulary	

Comprehension— Read the following questions and statements. For each one, put an *x* in the box before the option that contains the most complete or accurate answer. Check your answers in the Answer Key on page 108.

1. Astro Velcro has been used in
   - ☐ a. baseball parks.
   - ☐ b. space shuttles.
   - ☐ c. army tanks.
   - ☐ d. artificial hearts.

2. Velcro works for the same reason that
   - ☐ a. car bumpers don't fall off.
   - ☐ b. trampolines are bouncy.
   - ☐ c. jigsaw puzzle pieces stick together.
   - ☐ d. cockleburs adhere to socks.

3. Georges deMestral invented Velcro after
   - ☐ a. many years of experimentation.
   - ☐ b. attending a conference in Holland.
   - ☐ c. talking with David Letterman.
   - ☐ d. taking a walk in the woods.

4. Velcro has
   - ☐ a. solved the problems of most manufacturers.
   - ☐ b. become a standing joke among manufacturers.
   - ☐ c. revolutionized the design of many products.
   - ☐ d. made its inventor very wealthy.

5. The original patent for Velcro prevented
   - ☐ a. lawsuits.
   - ☐ b. imitations.
   - ☐ c. accidents.
   - ☐ d. misunderstandings.

6. The invention of Velcro has been
   - ☐ a. unimportant.
   - ☐ b. of questionable value.
   - ☐ c. beneficial to many people.
   - ☐ d. harmful to users.

7. Before Velcro was invented, blood pressure cuffs were
   - ☐ a. nonexistent.
   - ☐ b. held together with nails.
   - ☐ c. more difficult to fasten.
   - ☐ d. dangerous to use.

8. The author's suggestion for Edible Velcro is
   - ☐ a. hopeful.
   - ☐ b. rueful.
   - ☐ c. humorous.
   - ☐ d. insensitive.

9. Georges deMestral was
   - ☐ a. forgetful.
   - ☐ b. charming.
   - ☐ c. trustworthy.
   - ☐ d. observant.

10. Two examples of alliteration can be found in the selection:
   - ☐ a. sticky subject, secret sauce
   - ☐ b. mooshoo shoot, burrito squirt
   - ☐ c. womb-to-tomb, hook-and-loop
   - ☐ d. flimsy pancakes, titanium rivets

Comprehension Skills	
1. recalling specific facts	6. making a judgment
2. retaining concepts	7. making an inference
3. organizing facts	8. recognizing tone
4. understanding the main idea	9. understanding characters
5. drawing a conclusion	10. appreciation of literary forms

Study Skills, Part One—Following is a passage with blanks where words have been omitted. Next to the passage are groups of five words, one group for each blank. Complete the passage by selecting the correct word for each of the blanks.

Using Specialized Lists

You will naturally want your lists of specialized terms to be readily accessible and easy to use when you ___(1)___ them. There are different ways to accomplish this.

Some students list each word on its own 3 × 5 card along with the definition and an explanation. The cards can be filed alphabetically or by unit. Words recorded in this fashion are easily ___(2)___, located, and reviewed.

Others prefer to use their notebooks. This arrangement

(1)		finish		see
	need		lose	find

(2)		signaled		sorted
	diffused		collected	researched

allows new terms to be recorded close to the __(3)__ accompanying the lecture or chapter where the new terms were first used. Words cataloged this way make reviewing easier since you are able to use your knowledge of the terms as an aid to recall important concepts from the lecture or text.

Each night new terms should be studied during the __(4)__ and memorization segment of your study period. The words will then be fresh in your mind for class the following day.

Periodically (__(5)__ midterm examinations, for example), all specialized terms should be reviewed and studied. It is prudent at this time to attempt to write the definition of each term from memory. It is important to recall the exact wording since precise definitions are more useful to you both in understanding the subject matter and for __(6)__ your understanding to your instructor.

Studying word lists is not the only method of developing __(7)__ .

Other ways include using contextual aids and studying word roots, prefixes, and suffixes.

(3)	notes	illustrations
	bibliography index	suggestions
(4)	learning	preparation
	review experimentation	presentation
(5)	after	during
	following before	replacing
(6)	disguising	delivering
	defending deducting	demonstrating
(7)	phonics	vocabulary
	inference scholarship	judgment

Study Skills, Part Two—Read the study skills passage again, paying special attention to the lesson being taught. Then, without looking back at the passage, complete each sentence below by writing in the missing word or words. Check the Answer Key on page 108 for the answers to Study Skills, Part One, and Study Skills, Part Two.

1. Index cards enable students to file new words _____ or by unit.

2. Words listed in the student's _____ can also be readily available.

3. New terms should be _____ each night.

4. Periodically, the student should attempt to write the definition of each term

   from _____ .

5. _____ definitions are more useful for understanding subject matter.

15 | **Marilyn: An Untold Story**

by Norman Rosten

Vocabulary—The five words below are from the story you are about to read. Study the words and their meanings. Then complete the ten sentences that follow, using one of the five words to fill in the blank in each sentence. Mark your answer by writing the letter of the word on the line before the sentence. Check your answers in the Answer Key on page 108.

A. eminent: prominent

B. ominous: threatening; menacing

C. converged: came together

D. apprehensive: uneasy; anxious

E. effusive: emotionally unrestrained

_____ 1. Marilyn's _____ admirers showed little respect for her privacy.

_____ 2. The author sensed something _____ in the pack of teenagers surrounding Marilyn on the beach.

_____ 3. Even the _____ Khrushchev admired Marilyn.

_____ 4. The paths of Marilyn Monroe and Arthur Miller _____ more than once.

_____ 5. Marilyn seemed _____ about swimming in the ocean.

_____ 6. The public was _____ in its praise of Marilyn.

_____ 7. As he took Marilyn out into deeper water, the author heard the _____ cries of the mob.

_____ 8. A bra company was looking for an _____ actress to model its product.

_____ 9. Marilyn did not seem at all _____ about posing in the nude.

_____ 10. Initially Marilyn did not seem disturbed by the crowd that _____ around the umbrella.

That spring seemed a happy time in her life. She had met new friends in New York; she found a new analyst; she began attending the Actors Studio and taking private acting lessons from its eminent director, Lee Strasberg. And the most crucial event: She had renewed her acquaintance with Arthur Miller to whom she had been casually introduced earlier in Hollywood.

I was driving her out to our rented summer place on the north shore of Long Island, two hours from New York. It was then, for the first time, that I realized the extent of her fame. This time, everyone recognized her.

She sensed love as the hidden miracle in the human scheme.

With the roof down, visible as hell, she was a blinking buoy, a sweet-sounding siren, a magnetic field. People waved and shouted from passing cars as we crossed the 59th Street Bridge. "Hi, Marilyn! Hello, Marilyn! Hey, good luck! Is that you, Marilyn? Love you!" And she waved back, sipping champagne from a paper cup. (The chilled bottle nesting in the glove compartment and several others tucked away in the trunk.)

I was grimly trying to shake these admirers.

"Cheer up," she said, laughing. "They won't hurt us."

"You mean they won't hurt *you*," I replied. "The last guy who waved looked like he wanted to lynch *me*."

The sun blazed overhead. The car sped along. She sipped the champagne in silence, then said, "It scares me. All those people I don't know, sometimes they're so emotional. I mean if they love you that much without knowing you, they can also hate you the same way."

As a summer weekend house guest, she fit in well with the family. On the surface, cheerful and cooperative. She helped cook, prepare spaghetti, and open the clams, and always volunteered to do the dishes. She was especially proud of her dishwashing and held up the glasses for inspection, explaining she had more experience than anyone at washing dishes from the foster homes of her childhood. It was both a reminder and a disclaimer of her "waif" past. Champagne was another gesture of emancipation. Champagne and caviar were the very opposite of waifdom. Each popping cork proclaimed: Look at me, this is no abandoned child, no orphan!

She played badminton with a real flair, once banging friend Ettore Rella on the head (no damage). She was relaxed, giggling, tender.

She liked her guest room; she'd say, nodding for the shade to be drawn at bedtime, "Make it dark and give me air." She slept late, got her own breakfast, and went off for a walk in the woods with only the cat for company.

Her summer visits were not always restful. Everywhere she went, there was a potential scene. Because anything could happen with her around, wherever it was. Explosion. No match, just her and air. Spontaneous combustion. We

had some close calls. One of these still gives me a small sweat to this day. (In retrospect, all adventures with Marilyn had this unpredictable, ominous side, as though she were thumbing her nose at fate. She and fate always seemed to be side-stepping one another; I think fate was a little scared of her.)

It happened on the beach. Deserted area. Small group, big umbrella. Champagne from the trunk compartment of the car, neatly packed in dry ice. I will not attempt to describe her bathing suit except to say I have a photo of her in that suit I look at when the poetry is going bad and I need a charge.

Two stringy boys, idly paddling by in a camp canoe, saw her, edged closer for a look, and sped away with the news. As though a colony of ants had been activated, teen-agers began to file past us, first in wide circles around our party, then moving in closer, and finally about fifty worshipers converged upon the umbrella under which she demurely sat. She rose to greet them.

"Hey, Marilyn, I see all your movies!"

"You're my favorite!"

"You look terrific!"

"Marilyn, how about a kiss!"

She shook their hands and joked with them. They brought stones for her to autograph. The boys circled her tightly, the girls screamed, and a kind of panic set in. They reached for her with wild little cries, touching her, uttering pleas, begging favors while she laughed, fended them off as they slowly crowded her toward the water. Finally, the only escape was the water, and with an apprehensive wave, she started swimming. A barrage of cheers, and fifty tanned young bodies plunged in and gave chase.

Several of our group swam after her, trying to cut them off. They kept clamoring for Marilyn; she was surrounded.

"Hey," she called to me faintly. "Get me out of here!"

I managed to plough through to her side, shouting at the kids: "Beat it, get moving, go on home!" I struck at them blindly, furiously, and seizing her by the arm, started swimming out into deeper water. I threatened those hardier ones who followed; they watched us, grinning, as we plodded out.

Suddenly, Marilyn stopped.

"I can't swim any more," she pleaded.

"What do you mean, you can't."

"I'm not a good swimmer even when I'm good," she said.

"We can't turn back. Those vultures are waiting."

"You go back and let me die."

I saw the headlines: FILM STAR DROWNED. FRIEND IN FUTILE RESCUE ATTEMPT. SUICIDE PACT HINTED. She was breathing hard, her chin just above the water.

"Listen," I said. "Can you float? Try it. Take a deep breath and lean back." She tried but swallowed water and began to cough. I circled her, puffing a bit, and attempted to get her to lie back on the water. "Boy, what a way to go!" she gasped, clutching me. I thought of yelling for help, but if those kids swam out to help us, we'd drown for sure.

How else would we be saved if not by a Hollywood ending? The roar of a motor boat on the soundtrack. Real boat on wide-screen water. This crew-cut kid snakes up alongside, idles the motor. We both grabbed on to the side. I climbed into the boat, and there was the problem of hauling M. up over the side. She was rather dead weight by now, and she was not then nor had she ever been a thin slip of a girl. I finally pulled her up, and she fell heavily into the boat.

I looked at her as she lay exhausted, her legs curled up, her pink toes gleaming in the sun. The boy-pilot also regarded her with an adolescent's transfixed stare, forgetting the wheel and executing two tight circles before I realized what was happening. I shouted at him, and she said, "Don't be nervous, it's a wonderful weekend!"

That was the only time I had the chance to save her life.

She could give an appearance of toughness, and she could be tough. She knew the price—and paid it—of living in a professional world and industry dominated by men. She was engaged in a struggle to be herself. In the film industry women were chattel, packaged sex, decoys for the gullible public. On more than one occasion, Marilyn showed her independence. When she posed for the famous nude calendar—very daring in the early fifties—she defended it on the grounds that (1) she had to pay her rent, and it was honest work, and (2) the human body is nothing to be ashamed of (a sentiment that was to become the battle cry of Women's Liberation a decade later).

At the height of her fame, she was approached to model for a TV bra commercial. She turned it down contemptuously; she knew the difference between necessity and exploitation. But she had no qualms about wearing a dress without a stitch beneath it. One summer in the country, Hedda and she went shopping in Saks Fifth Avenue (Southampton). Marilyn was wearing a simple white cotton dress. A saleslady recognized her and with barely restrained excitement selected a half-dozen dresses for Marilyn to try on. In the dressing room the effusive saleslady said, "Let me help you," and unzipped the back of her dress, which fell to the floor. There stood Marilyn like Venus rising from that famous half shell. The saleslady, flustered, blushed. "Oh dear," she murmured, wondering perhaps if it was against the rules to try on Saks gowns over a nude body—even this famous one. But Marilyn blithely proceeded to try them. Perhaps because she noticed the saleslady's concern, she bought all six.

I suspect she would have quarreled with her sisters on the sex-liberation issue. In terms of economic equality with men, she had long proved herself. Certainly her problems in finding herself went far beyond and much deeper than the emancipation promises of Women's Liberation. She was very aware of herself as a woman and enjoyed her femininity, recognizing very well its power over others. However narcissistic or exhibitionist her feelings about herself, they were corroborated daily by the media and the masses of her admirers. Many women were drawn to her, probably more keenly aware than men of her extreme vulnerability; nor did they see her as a threat.

Marilyn sensed the difference in sexual psychology between men and women. She would tell of the time in Hollywood when Khrushchev, the Soviet premier, was being honored at a dinner. She was seated at a table in the audience (her studio had "demoted" her from the VIP dais) when Khrushchev passed by to shake her hand. "He didn't say anything," Marilyn recounted with pride. "He just looked at me. He looked at me the way a man looks on a woman. That's how he looked at me."

Marilyn was a true seductress. She didn't want to be considered a sex symbol or any symbol, but she enjoyed her role as a sexual person. She would laugh and say that to her a "cymbal" was something in an orchestra. She was an individual, and a woman. If men whistled at her, that was OK; if they were obscene, she knew how to handle it. She understood the carnal male syndrome and would never censure a man for beating the woman to the draw, so to speak. She enjoyed the idea of men desiring her; it amused, flattered, and excited her. She needed that proof of being adored; it denied the inner dread of being unwanted, the trauma of the illegitimate and motherless child. She sensed love as the hidden miracle in the human scheme. Love the great equalizer—if one were lucky enough to find it.

American movie actress Marilyn Monroe was admired by millions for her beauty and charm. Of her thirty films, her most successful roles were in *Bus Stop* (1956), and *The Misfits* (1961). She was married to former baseball star Joe DiMaggio in 1954, divorced the same year, and married to playwright Arthur Miller from 1956 to 1961. Despite her world fame and success in films, Monroe led a tragic life. In 1962, she died at age 36 from an overdose of sleeping pills.

Starting Time		Finishing Time	
Reading Time		Reading Rate	
Comprehension		Vocabulary	

Comprehension— Read the following questions and statements. For each one, put an *x* in the box before the option that contains the most complete or accurate answer. Check your answers in the Answer Key on page 108.

1. As a child, Marilyn had been
   □ a. abandoned.
   □ b. ugly.
   □ c. famous.
   □ d. rich.

2. Something about Marilyn seemed to
   □ a. produce conflict.
   □ b. encourage peace.
   □ c. inspire distrust.
   □ d. disturb women.

3. Marilyn asked the author for help when she
   □ a. ran out of champagne.
   □ b. met Arthur Miller.
   □ c. grew tired of swimming.
   □ d. went shopping in Saks Fifth Avenue.

4. Another title for this selection could be
   □ a. "Some Like It Hot."
   □ b. "A Star is Born."
   □ c. "What Price Glory?"
   □ d. "Games People Play."

5. A person in the public eye needs a
   □ a. pretty face.
   □ b. press agent.
   □ c. strong character.
   □ d. personal fortune.

6. From a publicity point of view, the drive to Long Island's north shore was
   □ a. disappointing.
   □ b. gratifying.
   □ c. embarrassing.
   □ d. uneventful.

7. The opening paragraph suggests a
   □ a. tragic ending.
   □ b. new beginning.
   □ c. disillusioned Marilyn.
   □ d. confused situation.

8. The author's treatment of this short chapter of Marilyn's life is
   □ a. sensitive and sympathetic.
   □ b. crude and contemptuous.
   □ c. daring and detailed.
   □ d. direct and factual.

9. Marilyn's attitude toward champagne and caviar demonstrated her basic
   □ a. insecurity.
   □ b. generosity.
   □ c. selfishness.
   □ d. optimism.

10. Which of the following sentences contains a cinematic allusion?
   □ a. "The roar of a motor boat on the soundtrack."
   □ b. "Those vultures are waiting."
   □ c. "They brought stones for her to autograph."
   □ d. "Love the great equalizer—if one were lucky enough to find it."

Comprehension Skills

1. recalling specific facts	6. making a judgment
2. retaining concepts	7. making an inference
3. organizing facts	8. recognizing tone
4. understanding the main idea	9. understanding characters
5. drawing a conclusion	10. appreciation of literary forms

Study Skills, Part One—Following is a passage with blanks where words have been omitted. Next to the passage are groups of five words, one group for each blank. Complete the passage by selecting the correct word for each of the blanks.

Other Word Study, I

1. Contextual Aids. By seeing a word in context, we come to know it better and better with every exposure. At first, the word becomes part of our ___(1)___ vocabulary. This means that we have seen it often enough to recognize it and remember its meaning. Many words remain just in our reading vocabulary. Other new words are repeated in

(1)   writing   speaking
        reading   specialized   general

print often enough for us to come to know them well; these words are then assimilated into our __(2)__ vocabulary. In effect, we are confident enough to use the word in our writing. When a word finally becomes totally __(3)__ , it may join our speaking vocabulary.

When read in context, words often have different shades of meaning that are imperceptible when initially read from a __(4)__ . A simple word like *root*, for example, has at least 22 different meanings. The word *perception* has very different meanings in law and in psychology. You can't even know how to pronounce *precedent*, let alone know its meaning, without seeing how it is being used. And the only way to avoid the __(5)__ between words like *precept* and *percept* is to learn them in context.

Further, relating a word to the way it is used increases our understanding not only of the word, but also of the idea the word represents. Consequently, words learned through context are more __(6)__ than those learned from lists.

2. Affixes and Roots. Still another kind of __(7)__ study centers around prefixes, suffixes, and roots. Because both prefixes and suffixes are added to words, they are collectively called affixes.

(2) writing   listening
    future   spelling   daily

(3) obscure   familiar
    forgotten   appreciated   analyzed

(4)   play   book
    list   sentence   magazine

(5) relationship   association
    friction   stress   confusion

(6) permanent   flexible
    temporary   definite   enjoyable

(7)   unit   sentence
    word   paragraph   chapter

Study Skills, Part Two—Read the study skills passage again, paying special attention to the lesson being taught. Then, without looking back at the passage, complete each sentence below by writing in the missing word or words. Check the Answer Key on page 108 for the answers to Study Skills, Part One, and Study Skills, Part Two.

1. Every time we see a word in context we get to know it _____ .

2. When we know a word completely it becomes part of our _____ vocabulary.

3. Some _____ of meaning are imperceptible when they are not read in context.

4. When we read a word in context we relate the word to the way it is _____ .

5. Prefixes and suffixes are both _____ to words.

16 | **The Open Window**

by Saki

Vocabulary—The five words below are from the story you are about to read. Study the words and their meanings. Then complete the ten sentences that follow, using one of the five words to fill in the blank in each sentence. Mark your answer by writing the letter of the word on the line before the sentence. Check your answers in the Answer Key on page 108.

A. endeavored: attempted

B. habitation: home; dwelling place

C. engulfed: swallowed up

D. ghastly: shockingly repellent; gruesome

E. convey: communicate

_____ 1. Mrs. Sappleton's niece told Framton a _____ story.

_____ 2. Framton _____ to make polite conversation with the niece.

_____ 3. Framton's new _____ was a rural retreat near the rectory.

_____ 4. Framton had apparently found his previous _____ hard on his nerves.

_____ 5. According to the niece, Mrs. Sappleton had been _____ by grief.

_____ 6. Framton had no opportunity to _____ his sympathy to Mrs. Sappleton.

_____ 7. As darkness _____ the rectory, Framton's attention was drawn to the open window.

_____ 8. The niece quickly _____ to explain Framton's hasty departure.

_____ 9. The aunt was unaware of the _____ tale Framton had been told.

_____ 10. Framton tried to _____ to Mrs. Sappleton the news about his illness.

"My aunt will be down presently, Mr. Nuttel," said a very self-possessed young lady of fifteen; "in the meantime you must try and put up with me."

Framton Nuttel endeavored to say the correct something which should duly flatter the niece of the moment without unduly discounting the aunt that was to come. Privately he doubted more than ever whether these formal visits on a succession of total strangers would do much toward helping the nerve cure which he was supposed to be undergoing.

"I know how it will be," his sister had said when he was preparing to migrate to this rural retreat; "you will bury yourself down there and not speak to a living soul, and your nerves will be worse than ever from moping. I shall just give you letters of introduction to all the people I know there. Some of them, as far as I can remember, were quite nice."

Framton wondered whether Mrs. Sappleton, the lady to whom he was presenting one of the letters of introduction, came into the nice division.

"Do you know many of the people round here?" asked the niece, when she judged that they had had sufficient silent communion.

"Hardly a soul," said Framton. "My sister was staying here, at the rectory, you know, some four years ago and she gave me letters of introduction to some of the people here."

He made the last statement in a tone of distinct regret.

"Then you know practically nothing about my aunt?" pursued the self-possessed young lady.

"Only her name and address," admitted the caller. He was wondering whether Mrs. Sappleton was in the married or widowed state. An undefinable something about the room seemed to suggest masculine habitation.

"Her great tragedy happened just three years ago," said the child; "that would be since your sister's time."

"Her tragedy?" asked Framton; somehow in this restful country spot tragedies seemed out of place.

"You may wonder why we keep that window wide open on an October afternoon," said the niece, indicating a large French window that opened onto a lawn.

"It is quite warm for the time of the year," said Framton; "but has that window got anything to do with the tragedy?"

"Out through that window, three years ago to a day, her husband and her two young brothers went off for their day's shooting. They never came back. In crossing the moor to their favorite snipe-shooting ground they were all three engulfed in a treacherous piece of bog. It had been that dreadful wet summer, you know, and places that were safe in other years gave way suddenly without warning. Their bodies were never recovered. That was the dreadful

Framton grabbed wildly at his stick and hat.

part of it." Here the child's voice lost its self-possessed note and became falteringly human. "Poor aunt always thinks that they will come back some day, they and the little brown spaniel that was lost with them, and walk in at that window just as they used to do. That is why the window is kept open every evening till it is quite dusk. Poor dear aunt, she has often told me how they went out, her husband with his white waterproof coat over his arm, and Ronnie, her youngest brother, singing, 'Bertie, why do you bound?' as he always did to tease her, because she said it got on her nerves. Do you know, sometimes on still, quiet evenings like this, I almost get a creepy feeling that they will all walk in through that window—"

She broke off with a little shudder. It was a relief to Framton when the aunt bustled into the room with a whirl of apologies for being late in making her appearance.

"I hope Vera has been amusing you?" she said.

"She has been very interesting," said Framton.

"I hope you don't mind the open window," said Mrs. Sappleton briskly; "my husband and brothers will be home directly from shooting, and they always come in this way. They've been out for snipe in the marshes today, so they'll make a fine mess over my poor carpets. So like you menfolk, isn't it?"

She rattled on cheerfully about the shooting and the scarcity of birds, and the prospects for duck in the winter. To Framton it was all purely horrible. He made a desperate but only partially successful effort to turn the talk on to a less ghastly topic; he was conscious that his hostess was giving him only a fragment of her attention, and her eyes were constantly straying past him to the open window and the lawn beyond. It was certainly an unfortunate coincidence that he should have paid his visit on this tragic anniversary.

"The doctors agree in ordering me complete rest, an absence of mental excitement, and avoidance of anything in the nature of violent physical exercise," announced Framton, who labored under the tolerably widespread delusion that total strangers and chance acquaintances are hungry for the least detail of one's ailments and infirmities, their cause and cure. "On the matter of diet they are not so much in agreement," he continued.

"No?" said Mrs. Sappleton, in a voice which only replaced a yawn at the last moment. Then she suddenly brightened into alert attention—but not to what Framton was saying.

"Here they are at last!" she cried. "Just in time for tea, and don't they look as if they were muddy up to the eyes!"

Framton shivered slightly and turned toward the niece with a look intended to convey sympathetic comprehension. The child was staring out through the open window with dazed horror in her eyes. In a chill shock of nameless fear Framton swung round in his seat and looked in the same direction.

In the deepening twilight three figures were walking across the lawn toward the window; they all carried guns under their arms, and one of them additionally burdened with a white coat hung over his shoulders. A tired brown spaniel kept close at their heels. Noiselessly they neared the house, and then a hoarse young voice chanted out of the dusk: "I said, Bertie, why do you bound?"

Framton grabbed wildly at his stick and hat; the hall door, the gravel drive, and the front gate were dimly noted stages in his headlong retreat. A cyclist coming along the road had to run into the hedge to avoid imminent collision.

"Here we are, my dear," said the bearer of the white mackintosh, coming in through the window; "fairly muddy, but most of it's dry. Who was that who bolted out as we came up?"

"A most extraordinary man, a Mr. Nuttel," said Mrs. Sappleton; "could only talk about his illness, and dashed off without a word of good bye or apology when you arrived. One would think he had seen a ghost."

"I expect it was the spaniel," said the niece calmly; "he told me he had a horror of dogs. He was once hunted into a cemetery somewhere on the banks of the Ganges by a pack of pariah dogs, and had to spend the night in a newly dug grave with the creatures snarling and grinning and foaming just above him. Enough to make anyone lose their nerve."

Romance at short notice was her specialty.

H. H. Munro is a British writer who wrote under the pen name Saki. He is best known for his many witty short stories and his satirical writings about British society of the early 1900s. Born in Akyab, Burma, in 1870, Munro came to England when he was two years old and later became a well-known London journalist. In 1916 he was killed in a battle in France during World War I.

Starting Time		Finishing Time	
Reading Time		Reading Rate	
Comprehension		Vocabulary	

Comprehension— Read the following questions and statements. For each one, put an *x* in the box before the option that contains the most complete or accurate answer. Check your answers in the Answer Key on page 108.

1. When Framton saw the hunters approaching the open window, he
   - ☐ a. fainted.
   - ☐ b. grabbed his white coat.
   - ☐ c. ran out of the house.
   - ☐ d. stared at the brown spaniel.

2. The purpose of Framton's visit to the country was to
   - ☐ a. convalesce.
   - ☐ b. investigate.
   - ☐ c. study.
   - ☐ d. hunt.

3. This was Framton's
   - ☐ a. first visit to Mrs. Sappleton.
   - ☐ b. second visit to Mrs. Sappleton.
   - ☐ c. third visit to Mrs. Sappleton.
   - ☐ d. fourth visit to Mrs. Sappleton.

4. Framton was
   - ☐ a. constantly disappointed by people.
   - ☐ b. the victim of a cruel joke.
   - ☐ c. struggling to maintain his sanity.
   - ☐ d. unable to take people at their word.

5. Throughout the story Mrs. Sappleton is
   - ☐ a. obviously strange.
   - ☐ b. obviously irritated.
   - ☐ c. perfectly normal.
   - ☐ d. understandably sad.

6. Which of the following is calculated to support the reader's first impression of Mrs. Sappleton?
   - ☐ a. "Just in time for tea, and don't you think they look as if they were muddy up to the eyes."
   - ☐ b. "A most extraordinary man, a Mr. Nuttel."
   - ☐ c. "One would think he had seen a ghost."
   - ☐ d. "I expect it was the spaniel."

7. After meeting Mrs. Sappleton for the first time, Framton must have
   - ☐ a. envied her husband.
   - ☐ b. felt at ease.
   - ☐ c. thought her strange.
   - ☐ d. wanted to stay.

8. Interpreted in the light of the entire story, which of the following comments is humorous?
   - ☐ a. ". . . you will bury yourself out there . . ."
   - ☐ b. "It is quite warm for the time of the year."
   - ☐ c. "I hope Vera has been amusing you?"
   - ☐ d. "Her great tragedy happened just three years ago."

9. At first, Mrs. Sappleton's niece seems to be
   - ☐ a. nervous and suspicious.
   - ☐ b. bold and fearless.
   - ☐ c. timid and retiring.
   - ☐ d. confident and alert.

10. The story has
    - ☐ a. abnormal characters.
    - ☐ b. a surprise ending.
    - ☐ c. a mysterious setting.
    - ☐ d. a complicated plot.

Comprehension Skills

1. recalling specific facts	6. making a judgment
2. retaining concepts	7. making an inference
3. organizing facts	8. recognizing tone
4. understanding the main idea	9. understanding characters
5. drawing a conclusion	10. appreciation of literary forms

Study Skills, Part One—Following is a passage with blanks where words have been omitted. Next to the passage are groups of five words, one group for each blank. Complete the passage by selecting the correct word for each of the blanks.

Other Word Study, II

When a prefix is added to the beginning of a word, it causes a change in the ___(1)___ of that word. For example, the prefix *un-*, when added to a word like *happy,* gives the word a completely opposite meaning.

Suffixes are added to the ends of words. Although they do not affect the basic meaning of a word, suffixes frequently alter its part of speech. For example, a verb, *hate,* can become an ___(2)___ , *hateful,* when a suffix is added.

Word roots are often Latin and Greek ___(3)___ on which many of our English words are based. *Bio,* which means *life,* is a Greek root word. From it we get such English words as *biology, antibiotic,* etc.

Through the study of affixes and roots, you can get a better "feel" for the meaning of many new words. Understanding how a word has ___(4)___ its particular meaning makes it much more likely that the word will become a part of your vocabulary. Check each new word you encounter in a good dictionary. The origin of the root of the word is usually ___(5)___ .

As you become more familiar with words—their origins (etymology), and their formative parts—you will find that new and ___(6)___ words will be much less discouraging when you meet them.

Effective word use distinguishes the educated person. Throughout life, we are judged and ___(7)___ on the basis of our ability to communicate. Since you have the opportunity now to develop your vocabulary, start at once by using the means suggested in this selection and make words the servants of your mind.

(1)	appearance	pronunciation
	meaning	spelling	value

(2)	interjection	adverb
	adjective	exclamation	addition

(3)	stems	branches
	customs	stories	beliefs

(4)	lost	acquired
	changed	enriched	collected

(5)	avoided	omitted
	mentioned	translated	explained

(6)	encouraging	difficult
	irritating	appealing	effective

(7)	adopted	rejected
	evaluated	evicted	sentenced

Study Skills, Part Two—Read the study skills passage again, paying special attention to the lesson being taught. Then, without looking back at the passage, complete each sentence below by writing in the missing word or words. Check the Answer Key on page 108 for the answers to Study Skills, Part One, and Study Skills, Part Two.

1. A prefix is added to the _____ of a word

2. A suffix is added to the _____ of a word.

3. Word roots are often _____ on words of Greek or Latin origin.

4. To discover the origin of a word, one should consult a good _____ .

5. Effective word use distinguishes the _____ person.

17 | Henry Ford's Fabulous Flivver

by Irwin Ross

Vocabulary—The five words below are from the story you are about to read. Study the words and their meanings. Then complete the ten sentences that follow, using one of the five words to fill in the blank in each sentence. Mark your answer by writing the letter of the word on the line before the sentence. Check your answers in the Answer Key on page 108.

A. obsolescent: outdated

B. attributes: features; qualities

C. placate: pacify; appease

D. dubiously: skeptically

E. castigated: criticized; chastized

_____ 1. Other companies produced cars with such _____ as gearshifts and lively colors.

_____ 2. Henry Ford did not want his cars to become _____ .

_____ 3. Some people _____ Ford for not producing cars in different colors.

_____ 4. Henry Ford's new car was designed to _____ his critics.

_____ 5. Some popular jokes emphasized the Model T's most endearing _____ .

_____ 6. Modern travelers would probably regard the flivver's magneto _____ .

_____ 7. Today's cars quickly become _____ .

_____ 8. Model T fans _____ the Ford Motor Company for its decision to discontinue the Model T.

_____ 9. Ford hoped the Model K would _____ investors.

_____ 10. Ford engineers viewed some proposed models _____ .

In this era of gaudy, expensive, annually obsolescent automobiles, it is difficult to realize that an American once grew rich by manufacturing the same car in the same model for 19 years. And the same color for 11 of those years.

The man was Henry Ford and the car was his remarkable Model T.

A unique motor car, the Model T held its own against Detroit's best for 19 years.

It was an odd-looking contraption, seven feet tall from top to pavement, as ungraceful as a village pump, as eccentric as the village hermit. It went its way making a noise like the end of the world. But it wrought prodigious changes in our nation's living; it was a revolution on wheels.

The Model T Ford—more familiarly referred to as the "flivver," "Tin Lizzie," or the "Leaping Lena"—made its debut in 1908. By 1927, when he finally discontinued it, Henry Ford had produced more than 15 million Model Ts. This was as many cars as had been turned out by all other automobile companies put together.

Where Mr. Ford's competitors issued new models every year, the Model T remained largely unchanged. There were occasional improvements, but it kept its same strange, three-pedal floor-board (clutch pedal on the left; reverse pedal in the center; brake on the right). And it was an unvarying black. Thus the famous quote by Mr. Ford:

"A customer can have a car painted any color he wants, so long as it is black."

But black had a reason. In the beginning, the touring model was painted red or a silver gray called "French Gray" and trimmed in highly polished brass. Then in 1914, Henry Ford began making cars on a fast production line basis that kept the cost low. The only color that would dry fast enough to keep the line moving was black Japan enamel. It wasn't until 1926 and 1927, the last two years of production, that colors were again made available.

The Model T had other quaint characteristics. On the touring car there was no left-hand door—only the outline of one stamped into the metal. There was no water pump. When the engine overheated, you lifted the sides of the hood and folded them under. This, as one person described it, gave the car the "appearance of a hen with her wings akimbo." There was no gas gauge. To find out how much fuel you had, you got out of the car, removed the front seat, unscrewed the gas cap beneath it and thrust in a stick or a ruler.

The lights of the Model T operated, not on a battery, but on a magneto (introduced after 1914), and glowed or faded according to the speed of the engine. If you became lost at night and stopped to get your bearings, you had to race your engine for enough light to read a sign or peer up the road ahead.

Starting a flivver was a massive test of patience, timing, and strength. You turned the ignition switch, jerked the spark down, shoved the accelerator up (in early models both were levers under the steering wheel), set the emergency brake, and walked resolutely to the front of the car. Pulling the choke wire which extended through the radiator, you grabbed the crank and gave it a hearty spin. If the engine caught, you raced back and jerked the accelerator down again before your snorting, quivering mount shook itself to pieces.

Yet with all its eccentricities, the Model T had three hugely endearing attributes. It was cheap (as low as $265 at one time). It was easy to drive. And it was durable. "She may not be pretty," flivver owners conceded, "but she gets you there and she brings you back."

A farmer wrote to the Ford factory that he had bought a secondhand Model T roadster two years old. He used it for 13 years as a farm truck, never had to overhaul it, put it in a repair shop only twice, and spent just $40 on mechanical upkeep.

Henry Ford was in the automobile business five years before he started producing the Model T. He had begun, logically, with the Model A, a two-cylinder car generating eight horsepower. He went from that to the four-cylinder Model B and on through the alphabet, although some of the models got no further than the drawing board.

Model K, when it came along, almost broke the infant Ford Motor Company. To placate stockholders who thought cars were only for the rich, Mr. Ford priced the Model K at $2,750—and had to sell every one at a loss.

This experience stiffened his determination to produce a cheap car. In due course, there emerged from his factory in the Highland Park suburb of Detroit, a Ford known as the Model T. As one student of the era has since observed, "That car had integrity. Perhaps nothing in it was beautiful—but nothing in it was false."

Standardized parts, mass-produced, were a prime reason for the cheapness of the Model T. You could buy a muffler for $2, a front fender for $6, a carburetor for $6. Model T parts were available almost everywhere—including five-and-ten-cent-stores.

But the marvel of the Model T was its planetary transmission. There was no gearshift to be jiggled until, with grinding and snarling, you slipped into gear. All you did was push the clutch pedal nearly to the floor, which put you in low gear, and gave her the gas. When you were hurtling along at 20 miles an hour, you released the clutch to go into high. For reverse, you depressed the center pedal. A youngster could do it.

Attracted by their simplicity as well as their economy, people bought flivvers in droves. For a long time Mr. Ford couldn't make enough of them to supply the demand. From 1918 to 1923, although local Ford dealers advertised, Mr. Ford disdained to do so. He didn't have to.

And so the flivver proliferated. One wisecrack of the period was: "Two flies can manufacture 48,876,552,154 new flies in six months, but they haven't anything on two Ford factories." Model Ts rattled through the towns and cities and along the country roads. Farmers installed tractor wheels and did their plowing with Model Ts. They jacked up the rear end, removed a tire, attached a belt, and ran buzz saws, pumped water, churned butter, ground feed, and generated electricity. Railroads put flanged wheels on Model Ts and used them as inspection cars. Movie companies made Model Ts collapsible and used them in the Keystone Cop comedies.

In the wake of its popularity there sprang up a whole school of Model T humor:

"Why is a Ford like a bathtub?"

"You hate to be seen in one."

"Didja know that Ford's going to paint his cars yellow so they can be hung outside of grocery stores and sold in bunches like bananas?"

"Heard the one about the farmer? He stripped the tin roof off his barn, sent it to Ford, and got back a letter saying, "While your car was an exceptionally bad wreck, we will be able to complete repairs and return it by the end of the week!"

These Model T jokes grew so plentiful that ultimately they were anthologized into books.

Henry Ford told the stories himself and plainly recognized that Model T jokes—complimentary or otherwise—were fine free publicity. One of his own favorite stories concerned the time he was traveling in a Ford car, inspecting some Michigan lumber properties with several aides. They came onto a farmer who was having trouble with his automobile—a beaten-up Ford. Mr. Ford and his men stopped, went to work on the car and, after replacing some spark plugs, got it running again.

"How much do I owe you fellers?" asked the farmer.

"Nothing," said Henry Ford rolling down his sleeves.

The farmer looked at him dubiously. "Can't make you out," he puzzled. "You talk as if money didn't mean anything to you, but if you've got so much money, why are you running around in a Ford?"

Henry Ford did indeed make a lot of money out of the Model T. He became, in fact, one of the two or three wealthiest men in the world. Moreover, the Model T brought fantastic returns to his original stockholders before he bought them all out. In all, $28,000 was invested in the Ford Motor Company by 12 people, and in ten years they made back a quarter-billion.

Henry Ford castigated competitors who brought out new models every year. "It does not please us to have a buyer's car wear out or become obsolete," he said. "We want the man who buys one of our products never to have to buy another."

But in the mid-1920s, the flivver began to encounter sales resistance. Other makes, with their gearshifts, accessories, lively colors, and annual model changes, were catching the fancy of the public. Mr. Ford blamed the Model T's loss of popularity on almost everything except the Model T. He said that the dealers' "mental attitude" was bad. He said that the American people had "fallen under the spell of salesmanship." But at last, reluctantly, he agreed that the Model T had to give way to mechanical progress.

The whole nation waited in tingling suspense for news of the new Ford. When the new car appeared with stylish lines and in different colors, it made the front page of practically every newspaper in the United States. And with it came one final Ford joke: "Henry's made a lady out of Lizzie."

Not everyone greeted the changeover with great joy. When an elderly woman in New Jersey heard that the Model Ts were being discontinued, she bought seven of them and stored them away so she would have Model Ts for the rest of her life and never have to change.

On May 26, 1927, the 15 millionth Model T rolled off the assembly line. Shortly afterward production of the phenomenal flivvers stopped entirely. An era had ended.

Starting Time		Finishing Time	
Reading Time		Reading Rate	
Comprehension		Vocabulary	

Comprehension— Read the following questions and statements. For each one, put an *x* in the box before the option that contains the most complete or accurate answer. Check your answers in the Answer Key on page 108.

1. The first car Henry Ford built had
   - ☐ a. two cylinders.
   - ☐ b. four cylinders.
   - ☐ c. six cylinders.
   - ☐ d. eight cylinders.

2. The automobile
   - ☐ a. changed America's lifestyle.
   - ☐ b. was a hazard to livestock.
   - ☐ c. threatened the American economy.
   - ☐ d. was a familiar sight in the early days.

3. From 1918 to 1923, Henry Ford
   - ☐ a. experimented with different types of Model Ts.
   - ☐ b. lost millions with his Model K.
   - ☐ c. produced red and gray touring cars.
   - ☐ d. didn't bother to advertise his product.

4. The public in Mr. Ford's day appreciated
   - ☐ a. luxury and versatility.
   - ☐ b. speed and safety.
   - ☐ c. economy and durability.
   - ☐ d. style and color.

5. Owners and drivers of the Model T had to be
   - ☐ a. wealthy and educated.
   - ☐ b. influential.
   - ☐ c. patient and resourceful.
   - ☐ d. uncaring.

6. Henry Ford's early domination of the automotive industry resulted from
   - ☐ a. daring financial investments.
   - ☐ b. a proud family tradition.
   - ☐ c. questionable business techniques.
   - ☐ d. a successful formula.

7. In the early days of the automobile, Henry Ford was the
   - ☐ a. only producer of automobiles.
   - ☐ b. controlling force in the stock market.
   - ☐ c. main supporter of labor unions.
   - ☐ d. major manufacturer of automobiles.

8. Henry Ford's statement that he didn't want his cars to become obsolete was
   - ☐ a. sarcastic.
   - ☐ b. ironic.
   - ☐ c. sincere.
   - ☐ d. sorrowful.

9. Henry Ford believed in giving consumers
   - ☐ a. a host of options.
   - ☐ b. an honest value.
   - ☐ c. occasional gifts.
   - ☐ d. detailed instructions.

10. The selection is written in the form of a
   - ☐ a. conversation.
   - ☐ b. short story.
   - ☐ c. historical essay.
   - ☐ d. narrative.

Comprehension Skills

1. recalling specific facts	6. making a judgment
2. retaining concepts	7. making an inference
3. organizing facts	8. recognizing tone
4. understanding the main idea	9. understanding characters
5. drawing a conclusion	10. appreciation of literary forms

Study Skills, Part One—Following is a passage with blanks where words have been omitted. Next to the passage are groups of five words, one group for each blank. Complete the passage by selecting the correct word for each of the blanks.

Listening Effectively

A wise man once said that listening is the hardest thing in the world to do. Today, listening is a lost art for most people. Understanding listening faults is a prerequisite to overcoming them. Suggestions for improving listening help you to ___(1)___ poor habits and cultivate good ones.

Faulty listening leads to ___(2)___ , and that can be the cause of many problems. There are those who feel, with good reason, that we might have universal peace if only people would really listen to one ___(3)___ .

In industry, millions of dollars are lost annually as a result of poor listening. Consequently, it has become standard practice at most major companies to "write it down." Xerox, a leading corporation, has developed an employee listening improvement course that it now sells to other countries.

In school, many students fail to listen properly to instructions. After many exams we hear about those who lose credit because they did not follow ___(4)___ .

(1)   compound   correct   improve   recognize   create

(2)   misunderstanding   comprehension   communication   anxiety   boredom

(3)   another   person   theory   group   alone

(4)   distractions   ideas   directions   attitudes   assignments

LISTENING FAULTS

One of the causes of faulty listening is daydreaming. This is probably the most troublesome listening fault because it affects almost everyone. Frequently a speaker will mention some person or thing that triggers an ___(5)___ in our minds and we begin to daydream. When we return to reality and begin listening again, we discover that point three is now being presented and we have no ___(6)___ of points one and two.

Opportunities for daydreaming are abundant because people speak at a much slower rate than we can ___(7)___ . Thus, when a speaker is talking at a rate of 125 words-a-minute, the listener's mind may wander off.

(5)	inspiration		order
	activity	actuality	association

(6)	relation		organization
	recollection	admiration	recognition

(7)	expect		imagine
	listen	think	dream

Study Skills, Part Two—Read the study skills passage again, paying special attention to the lesson being taught. Then, without looking back at the passage, complete each sentence below by writing in the missing word or words. Check the Answer Key on page 108 for the answers to Study Skills, Part One, and Study Skills, Part Two.

1. Misunderstanding is caused by _____ listening.

2. In _____ , poor listening causes a loss of millions of dollars annually.

3. In school, students often lose _____ in exams as a result of poor listening.

4. Daydreaming is a fault that affects almost _____ .

5. A speaker will often mention something that will trigger an association in our minds and cause us to _____ .

18 | Golden Oldies

by Willard Scott

Vocabulary—The five words below are from the story you are about to read. Study the words and their meanings. Then complete the ten sentences that follow, using one of the five words to fill in the blank in each sentence. Mark your answer by writing the letter of the word on the line before the sentence. Check your answers in the Answer Key on page 108.

A. gumption: boldness

B. bungling: inept

C. abide: tolerate

D. liable: likely; apt

E. incredulous: disbelieving

_____ 1. A person turning 100 years old is _____ to be congratulated on the "Today" show.

_____ 2. When the stewardess revealed that the woman on the Concorde was 93 years old, the author was _____ .

_____ 3. The author told about his _____ attempt to deliver a cake with 100 blazing candles on it.

_____ 4. The author was the first one with enough _____ to announce birthdays on national television.

_____ 5. Wherever the author goes, he is _____ to be recognized by fans.

_____ 6. Some people cannot _____ the thought of growing old.

_____ 7. Centenarians often have more spirit and more _____ than we expect.

_____ 8. Network executives were probably _____ when they learned the author's plans to announce birthdays on the air.

_____ 9. Not all people can _____ cigarette smoke.

_____ 10. The author admits that he is a _____ amateur when it comes to telling jokes.

Somebody smarter than I'll ever be once said that age is a matter of mind—if you don't mind, it doesn't matter. I am reminded of this all the time, and I am reminded of it again now as I sit down to write this. I am on the Concorde, heading across the Atlantic from London to New York. They tell me the whole trip will take just under 3½ hours, and there is a feisty old woman sitting in front of me who seems determined to keep eating and drinking for the duration. Her ticket cost her $5,000, and from the way she's going, it looks as if the price will just about cover her food and drink.

I asked a woman if in her 100 years she'd ever been bedridden, and she told me, "Oh, yes, thousands of times, and once in a buggy."

I first noticed her back at the airport—they've got a luxurious lounge at Heathrow for Concorde passengers—and she made four trips to the complimentary buffet table they'd had set out there, and then she stuffed her purse with four or five candy bars. Here, on the plane, she's already sampled everything on a roving cheese tray, and she's got a brandy set up next to her second gin and tonic. She even took a cigar from the flight attendant who offered them, and I confess I was mildly surprised when she didn't light up; instead she tucked it away in her purse, presumably for later.

I flagged down a passing stewardess. "This lady is incredible," I said. "How old is she?" I thought from the way she moved and carried herself maybe she was 65, perhaps 70; it's possible she was a terrific-looking 75.

"She's 93," the stewardess answered.

Ninety-three? At first I couldn't believe it. I mean, this old lady had the spirit, fight, and gumption of a woman half her age. But then I stopped to think about it, and I wasn't really surprised at all. More and more I hear incredible stories about the most senior of our country's senior citizens, and what was once disbelief on my part has turned to sheer wonder. Talk about amazing stories! Steven Spielberg could learn a thing or three from the tens of thousands of centenarians who were born long before the very idea of color pictures (let alone moving ones) had caught on in this country.

When it comes to centuries-old traditions, there are none grander than the hundreds of men and women I am lucky enough to meet and congratulate on the occasions of their 100th birthdays. And from the looks of things, I'll have my work cut out for me in the years ahead.

Like every good thing that's ever happened to me in my career, my involvement with senior citizens happened almost by accident. It was a fluke, really; I just kind of backwarded myself into something that would change my whole life. Here's the story. About six years ago, a friend asked me to wish his Uncle Clarence a happy 100th birthday on the air, the sort of request I received all the time but always had to decline because of the perceived ethics of network news. But then it occurred to me—hey, somebody is turning 100; if that's not newsworthy, then I don't know what is. So I went against standard practice, against the advice of the network, and wished old Clarence good health and good wishes over the air. But there was no way to prepare for what happened next. I thought maybe I'd get the old hand slap for bucking the system, but instead what I got was a slow stream of similar requests. Actually, it started out as little more than a drip. (And if you asked some people, they'd tell you that's how I started out, too. Ba-dump-bump.) Two weeks later the drip turned to a trickle with two or three requests. I had struck a chord. Here was something—sending out birthday greetings across the miles to people who truly deserved a tip of the hat—that nobody else was doing. It was different. It was also folksy and homey and patriotic, and it fit me like a glove. And the network left me alone to do my thing. All because of Uncle Clarence, God bless him.

As for the birthday greetings themselves, they've quickly become an American tradition. My office has turned into this country's unofficial clearinghouse for soon-to-be centenarians. (There is also this place in Washington called the White House, perhaps you've heard of it, where they do a fine job of identifying and congratulating 100-year-olds in this country. But they've got to take care of some other business as well, and I am happily easing their burden in this area.) I'm known for my birthday greetings to the senior set more than anything else I've done in my 35 years in this business. Viewers of all ages, I think, are uplifted by my celebration of these grand old folks; there is a deep-seated respect for age in this country, a respect that cuts across all issues of race and social and economic class, and it seems I've plugged into something through which we can all draw quiet inspiration. Everywhere I go, people trot out an elderly relative they'd like me to meet. Once, when I was in Lansing, Michigan, a big yellow school bus pulled up to where we were doing our remote, and one of the kids stuck his head out the window and hollered, "Hey, Willard! Will you mention my birthday in 85 years?" I get reactions like this all the time, and it thrills me to see the kind of impact you can have through the power of television. It also keeps me humble.

Myron Cohen, the late, great borscht-belt comic, who himself lived to a ripe old age, used to tell a wonderful story about a 104-year-old man, a joke that bears repeating here. As Myron told the story, the old man stopped by his doctor's office one day for his annual checkup, and after being presented with a clean bill of health, he turned to the doctor and said, "See you next year."

"That's wonderful," said the doctor. "Not to alarm you

or anything, but here you are, 104 years old, and yet you're so confident you'll be healthy for another year. Tell me, how can you be so sure?"

"It has nothing to do with confidence," replied the old man in a thick, rich Yiddish accent, an accent I could never do justice to in person, let alone on paper. "It has to do with statistics, and statistics say that between the ages of 104 and 105, not too many people die."

I love that story. Not because it's side-splittingly funny (sometimes it doesn't even register a laugh when I tell it, although that probably has more to do with my bungling attempt at a thick, rich Yiddish accent than anything else), but because it speaks to a deeper truth about age and reason, about the keen insight and rare perspective you'll find among this country's only priceless antiques.

There are some wonderful jokes about old folks, but the funniest stories of all just happen to be true. Oh, I've met some terrific old characters on the road, folks we'd all love to have as our own crotchety old aunt or curmudgeonly uncle. Boy, can I tell you stories! Like the time I asked a woman if in her 100 years she'd ever been bedridden, and she told me, "Oh, yes, thousands of times, and once in a buggy, but don't you dare mention that on television." (I think she rehearsed that one.) Or the time a sweet old man took me aside and confided in me that he still likes the girls, although he said, "I can't exactly remember why." Then there's my favorite retired army colonel—Charles Norris of Charlotte, North Carolina— who told me how he can't abide the anxious stockbrokers who try to sell him on municipal bonds that won't mature for 20 years: "H___," he said, "at my age, I don't even buy green bananas."

Two of my favorite centenarian stories took place at the "Today" show. In the first, my celebration of the 100-plus set almost backfired and I mean literally backfired. We brought on a lovely man from New York City, a man who went to work every day up until his 100th birthday, and somebody got the bright idea of doing up a little birthday party after our interview. Well, this being morning television we trotted out a cake with 100 blazing birthday candles. Now, I don't know about you, but I'm not the sort of guy who should stand too close to 100 blazing candles, whether birthday or otherwise. One candle would have served quite nicely thank you very much. There I was, cake cradled cautiously in my arms, and the heat from the 100 candles started to melt the glue underneath my toupee. No kidding. Talk about a throw rug! I saw the tapes after the show, and you should have seen me struggle to hold on to the cake and to my store-bought hair with something resembling professional dignity. (Who knows, you're liable to see that clip turn up on one of those prime-time bloopers-and-blunders shows.) Now, whenever I'm wearing my ear-to-ear carpeting, I steer clear of birthday parties for anyone older than sweet 16!

The other "Today" show incident took place years before I arrived on the scene, but it's been passed on to me like an old family heirloom, so I'll just pass it along here. It seems that when the Surgeon General's office first issued its warnings on cigarette packages in the early 1960s, someone at NBC thought it would be a good idea to find an oldster with a lifelong smoking history; leave it to a TV newsman to play devil's advocate in these things. Well, somebody tracked down this 100-year-old man from down south, and NBC flew him to New York to appear on the show the next morning. When the producer of the show finally met the old man and explained the idea behind the segment, the old man started to shake his head as if he couldn't deliver.

"You mean to tell me you want me to get up at seven o'clock in the morning and tell a national television audience I've been smoking two packs of cigarettes a day since I was 12 years old?" the old man asked, incredulous.

"That's right," the producer said. "That's the truth, isn't it?"

"Of course it's the truth," the old man replied. "The trouble is I don't stop coughing until 11:30 at the earliest."

I never fail to get a laugh with that one.

I am always happily astonished by the spit and pluck of some of the old folks I am lucky enough to meet, even though I've seen and heard enough to leave me way past the point of wonder. I look over at this little old lady seated in front of me on the Concorde, this fireball with the appetite of an army, as she fidgets with the cigar she had packed away in her purse, and I wouldn't trade my seat for anything in the world. (I won't tell you whether or not she lit up—I am, after all, a gentleman—but I will tell you this: I flew back the rest of the way with a smile on my face and a song in my heart.)

Let me close this with my own variation on a popular birthday toast: may you all live to be 100, and when you get there may mine be the loudest voice of congratulations you hear.

Willard Scott is a radio and TV performer whose greatest fame has come as weather reporter for NBC's "Today" show. He received his B.A. in Philosophy and Religion from American University. His career in radio and TV spans 40 years, and includes stints on children's television shows, the Voice of NASA radio show, and a prime-time television comedy. He has also been active with many charities, including the March of Dimes, Easter Seals, and the American Cancer Society.

Starting Time		Finishing Time	
Reading Time		Reading Rate	
Comprehension		Vocabulary	

Comprehension — Read the following questions and statements. For each one, put an *x* in the box before the option that contains the most complete or accurate answer. Check your answers in the Answer Key on page 108.

1. Centenarians often receive official congratulations from
   - ☐ a. Myron Cohen.
   - ☐ b. the White House.
   - ☐ c. NBC executives.
   - ☐ d. flight attendants.

2. Many centenarians have
   - ☐ a. voracious appetites.
   - ☐ b. overwhelming physical problems.
   - ☐ c. a fine sense of humor.
   - ☐ d. no living relatives.

3. The first 100-year-old to be publicly congratulated by the author was
   - ☐ a. Charles Norris.
   - ☐ b. the woman on the Concorde.
   - ☐ c. Uncle Clarence.
   - ☐ d. Myron Cohen.

4. The author states that the old people in our society
   - ☐ a. are a tremendous burden on the young.
   - ☐ b. adore publicity.
   - ☐ c. appreciate even the smallest kindness.
   - ☐ d. deserve our respect.

5. The author has never regretted
   - ☐ a. wearing a toupee.
   - ☐ b. publicizing Clarence's birthday.
   - ☐ c. attending a birthday party.
   - ☐ d. his decision to become a smoker.

6. The author
   - ☐ a. performs a valuable service.
   - ☐ b. should not be taken seriously.
   - ☐ c. is an embarrassment to the NBC network.
   - ☐ d. appeals to sophisticated, adult viewers.

7. The author
   - ☐ a. thoroughly enjoys his job.
   - ☐ b. has many old relatives.
   - ☐ c. has a long-standing smoking habit.
   - ☐ d. used to be a stand-up comic.

8. The author writes about old people with
   - ☐ a. great warmth.
   - ☐ b. grudging admiration.
   - ☐ c. incredulity.
   - ☐ d. gratitude and humility.

9. The 93-year-old woman on the Concorde believed in
   - ☐ a. following social conventions.
   - ☐ b. sharing her good fortune.
   - ☐ c. tempting fate.
   - ☐ d. enjoying herself.

10. When the author says he had "a song in his heart," it means he was
    - ☐ a. nervous.
    - ☐ b. preoccupied.
    - ☐ c. happy.
    - ☐ d. awestruck.

Comprehension Skills

1. recalling specific facts	6. making a judgment
2. retaining concepts	7. making an inference
3. organizing facts	8. recognizing tone
4. understanding the main idea	9. understanding characters
5. drawing a conclusion	10. appreciation of literary forms

Study Skills, Part One — Following is a passage with blanks where words have been omitted. Next to the passage are groups of five words, one group for each blank. Complete the passage by selecting the correct word for each of the blanks.

Listening Faults

Closed-mindedness. We often refuse to listen to ideas and viewpoints that run __(1)__ to our preconceived notions about a subject. We say, in effect, "I know all I want to know, so there's no use listening."

Actually, this is an intellectual fault that leads to a listening problem. Closed-mindedness __(2)__ with

(1)   conclusive   parallel
        contrary   adjacent   similar

(2)   disagrees   consents
        intervenes   interferes   unites

learning by causing you to shut out facts you need to know whether you agree with them or not.

False Attention. This is a protective device that everyone resorts to from time to time. When we're not really interested in what a person has to say, we just ___(3)___ to listen. We nod and make occasional meaningless comments to give the ___(4)___ that we are paying attention, when actually our minds are elsewhere.

Intellectual Despair. Listening can be difficult at times. Often you must sit through lectures on subjects ___(5)___ to understand.

Obviously, you'll never understand if you give up. The thing to do is to listen more carefully than ever; ask questions when practical and, most important, discuss the material with a classmate. ___(6)___ the problem as soon as it appears. Catch up right away and you'll feel less inclined to adopt an attitude of futility.

Personality Listening. It is only natural for listeners to appraise and evaluate a speaker. Our impressions should not interfere with our listening, however. The content must be ___(7)___ on its own merits.

(3) proceed   pretend
refuse   offer   begin

(4) intention   concept
proof   impression   denial

(5) hard   unpleasant
easy   trivial   important

(6) Forget   Welcome
Ignore   Attack   Defend

(7) judged   overcome
enjoyed   rejected   accepted

Study Skills, Part Two—Read the study skills passage again, paying special attention to the lesson being taught. Then, without looking back at the passage, complete each sentence below by writing in the missing word or words. Check the Answer Key on page 108 for the answers to Study Skills, Part One, and Study Skills, Part Two.

1. _____ interferes with learning by causing you to shut out facts that you don't agree with.

2. False _____ is a protective device that we all use at one time or another.

3. If you do not understand something from a lecture, it is a good idea to _____ the material with a classmate.

4. The prompt solution of this problem prevents an attitude of _____ .

5. The speaker is less important than the _____ of the speech.

19 | When Pain is the Only Choice

by Elisabeth Rosenthal

Vocabulary—The five words below are from the story you are about to read. Study the words and their meanings. Then complete the ten sentences that follow, using one of the five words to fill in the blank in each sentence. Mark your answer by writing the letter of the word on the line before the sentence. Check your answers in the Answer Key on page 108.

A. caveat: warning

B. inure: harden

C. racked: tortured

D. insidious: spreading in a stealthy but harmful manner

E. alleviate: make less severe; reduce

_____ 1. During the weeks following chemotherapy, pain _____ Andrea's body.

_____ 2. Cancer is an _____ disease.

_____ 3. Part of a physician's job is to _____ suffering.

_____ 4. The medications that the doctors gave Andrea did little to _____ her pain.

_____ 5. To be effective, cancer specialists must _____ themselves to the pain of their patients.

_____ 6. A simple _____ about hair loss or mouth sores does not prepare a patient for chemotherapy.

_____ 7. It was difficult for the author to see Andrea _____ by fevers and nausea.

_____ 8. On the first day of treatment, a patient may not realize the _____ nature of radiation.

_____ 9. Doctors often issue a _____ before performing a painful procedure.

_____ 10. It was impossible for the author to _____ herself to Andrea's suffering.

A physician frequently observes suffering and even causes it in the name of healing. An inflamed gall bladder has to be surgically removed. A large tube is thrust into the chest cavity to remove infected fluid. A catheter is inserted through the neck into the heart in order to assess cardiac function. Each day

Are there times when even doctors cannot stand the pain they inflict on their patients?

I prod tender bellies and pierce bruised skin, with the glib caveat "this may hurt a bit." I know it does, but I also know I can't dwell on the pain if I am to do my job effectively.

Sometimes, however, pain and healing are so inextricably intertwined that even those of us who inure ourselves to suffering stand back in awe. My guard dropped when I treated my first bone marrow transplant patient.

Andrea was a young woman in her early thirties—about my age—who had just turned in her Ph.D. dissertation and was awaiting the results. Like other patients coming in for a bone marrow transplant, she arrived at the hospital as though embarking on a long journey to a strange and foreign land.

Intellectually Andrea knew what lay ahead of her. She expected to be in the hospital for weeks, if not months. Her body would be racked with lethal doses of radiation, then scourged by toxic chemicals. Her stay would almost certainly be punctuated by episodes of uncontrolled bleeding and infection.

She came prepared—in a sense. She unloaded a TV and ordered a VCR. She lined up Thomas Mann and Sartre on her bedside table. She clearly understood that her stay would be long and lonely, spent mostly in the confines of a 12-by-12-foot hospital room. But she had clearly chosen not to comprehend the prospect of her own suffering. A bone marrow transplant is not a good time to catch up on classics.

I saw no reason to press the issue. As I wrote her admission orders—instructions for chemo, instructions for radiation, pain meds, and more pain meds—we spoke instead about movies, books, the weather. We both tried to ignore my white coat. More to the point, we tried to ignore the tip of the catheter peeking out from the top of her nightdress. The catheter had been inserted into her chest to deliver blood products, drugs, and nutrition in the weeks to come.

As I rose to go I asked if she had any questions. Yes, she did. She had been told that her hair would fall out and that sores would form in her mouth that would make eating difficult. Was it true? "Yes," I answered, "I suppose these things generally happen." She shrugged her shoulders. It was best to focus on such tangible small details.

The logic of a bone marrow transplant is elegant and simple. While radiation and chemotherapy can effectively destroy tumor cells, use of these treatments is limited by the fact that they also kill certain normal cells—those of the hair follicles, those that line the intestines, and the so-called stem cells of the bone marrow. Of these, the bone marrow stem cells are the most sensitive to destruction and the most critical for life. When these cells mature they evolve into the white cells of the immune system, the red blood cells that carry oxygen from the lungs to the peripheral organs, and the platelets essential for blood coagulation. Without any one of these three, life is impossible.

Bone marrow transplants allow physicians to deliver very high doses of chemotherapy while sidestepping the problem of its toxic effect on marrow cells. Samples of the patient's own marrow or matched donor marrow are gathered and frozen weeks to months before the transplant. The marrow is harvested in the operating room through 100 to 150 deep needle sticks into the sternum or pelvis. The result is several small bags of red soupy material.

With the stem cells safely stored in the freezer, patients can proceed with radiation and chemotherapy. Their hair falls out, the lining of their gut disintegrates, and the bone marrow simply dies. Eventually their hair grows back, the intestines reline—and the marrow is replaced by those cells in plastic bags in the deep freeze.

The first few days of a marrow transplant are deceptively calm for all the destruction that is occurring. For five days running, Andrea was taken to the radiation therapy department to lie on a cold table, soaking up radiation comparable to that absorbed by those near the epicenter of Hiroshima. I recall asking Andrea if the radiation hurt.

"No," she said, "I don't feel anything." I knew this, but I still couldn't quite believe it. "I just feel very tired when they're done," she added.

What an insidious enemy! Millions of cells in her body in the throes of death, and no burn, no gash, no scar to show for it. Five days of this. Sartre never left the shelf.

Chemotherapy started on day four. As the high-dose Cytoxan and VP-16 flowed through her catheter line, Andrea experienced waves of nausea, which we vainly attempted to control with other medications. Soon after the chemotherapy ended, her body began slowly, subtly, to show the ravages of the battle raging inside. At first she complained only of some difficulty swallowing. The next day sores on her tongue and mucous membranes blossomed like fireworks. Similar lesions almost certainly extended deep into her esophagus, and soon she could not swallow at all for the pain. First no foods, then no liquids, then no pills—finally, not even her own saliva. Each day as she sat up to let me listen to her lungs, fistfuls of black hair remained on the white pillow.

My role quickly changed from peer to physician. As I entered her room I braced myself for the misery that would greet me.

"I'm in unbelievable pain."

"Where?" I would inquire, hoping desperately to discover some small source of discomfort I could potentially alleviate—a sty, an ingrown toenail, low back pain. "My mouth, my chest, my belly, everywhere. I can't bear it."

"I'll see if we can move up on your Dilaudid a bit," I said. (Andrea was already getting intravenous narcotics every three hours.) "And I'll get the mouth team to come by again and give you another spray." Her complaints were so pressing, and all I could offer her were Band-Aids.

Then, as predicted, Andrea's blood counts fell. The white blood cells that had formerly protected her body from infection slowly died, and her own marrow, poisoned by the chemotherapy, could not replace the loss. She became what is termed "absolutely neutropenic"— the concentration of bacteria-fighting white blood cells in her body was so low that she was at great risk of acquiring a life-threatening infection from the normally benign bacteria that live in our bathrooms, on tabletops, even on our skin and in our bodies.

From that point on, Andrea was placed in reverse isolation. The doctors and family members who entered her room wore mask, gown, and gloves for even minor social calls. She was not allowed gifts of fruits or flowers for fear they would carry a microbe that might kill her.

At last came the sound of the cavalry coming over the hill. The day of the transplant had arrived.

Transplant. I don't quite know what I expected. Drumrolls. Some drama, perhaps. As a medical student I had participated in a liver transplant. But the actual mechanics of a bone marrow transplant had never crossed my mind.

One morning just before lunch, as I was checking some X rays, I was paged to perform Andrea's "procedure." Her transplant would be done by me, at her bedside. Outside her room the senior oncologist was thawing the precious bags of marrow in a hot-water bath. As it reached body temperature he drew up the marrow into large 60-cubic-centimeter syringes and handed them to me.

I connected each syringe to the tubing of her catheter and began to push. The marrow was thick, and I met with more resistance than I had expected. But slowly the tubing blushed red and the vital marrow displaced the inconsequential IV fluid. In a minute or two the marrow cells had been forced into her veins. Andrea's urine turned red as she excreted waste products from the injected bone marrow. And then again, from the outside, all was quiet.

Andrea remained in the hospital for another difficult four months. Cardiac transplant patients look and feel better almost the day after surgery. They "pink up" as the new heart almost inevitably pumps blood better than the old. They smile. They pose for photos. For the bone marrow transplant patient the transplant is just a way station on a much longer journey.

Bone marrow cells take an average of two to four weeks before they begin to pour out the red cells, white cells, and platelets the body so sorely needs. Until the marrow recovers, the horrors progress.

Though we gowned and gloved religiously before entering her room, we couldn't completely protect Andrea from infection. She began to spike temps. First subtle temperatures: 99, 99.5. Then, within hours, real ragers: 103, 104. She shook like a leaf. We started broad spectrum antibiotics, and mercifully, the fevers calmed. Five days later, as they once again gained momentum, we mechanically added antifungal medication to her regimen. The medical profession has protocols for fighting the unknown. In this case they worked: the fever disappeared.

In its place came the bleeding. Andrea's platelet count had fallen steadily since her chemotherapy and it now hung tenuously around 10,000 (normal is greater than 150,000). Intermittently she would bleed: a nosebleed, a vaginal discharge, some bloody vomit. After one night of retching she was left with two impressive black eyes. The capillaries in the skin beneath her eyes had broken, the result of her blood pressure rising with diaphragmatic contractions when she vomited.

Two weeks after the transplant the person who greeted us in the morning bore little resemblance to the woman who had checked in: swollen jowls, black eyes, no hair, no spirit. The books were unopened, the TV was off. Her attention, understandably, was focused on herself—on the daily progress of her blood cell counts.

Gradually her marrow began to manufacture white cells and red cells of its own, and her blood counts began to rise. She went off antibiotics, and transfusions were no longer a nightly occurrence. But her platelet count remained disturbingly low and she continued to bleed. Met by her disappointment, I would remind her that after chemotherapy a cell line sometimes takes an unusually long time to recover.

Neither she nor I could utter the knowledge we shared: sometimes after a transplant the white cells or red cells or platelets never come back. For these patients, cured of cancer, life becomes a hellish wait for the ultimate infection or the ultimate bleed.

I hoped Andrea would not be one of the unlucky ones. I hoped she'd be one of those who leave the hospital hairless but triumphant.

Andrea finally did go home. Of the 11 patients who have received marrow transplants for Hodgkin's at my hospital, she is one of seven who are still alive. I too eventually left the bone marrow floor. As a resident in training it was time for me to move on to my next rotation in the cardiac care unit. Though it was difficult for me to watch Andrea's suffering, I remained convinced that for a patient like her a transplant still made sense. For myself, I was glad to return to a ward where the price of a cure in terms of suffering was not quite so high.

Starting Time		Finishing Time	
Reading Time		Reading Rate	
Comprehension		Vocabulary	

Comprehension

Comprehension— Read the following questions and statements. For each one, put an *x* in the box before the option that contains the most complete or accurate answer. Check your answers in the Answer Key on page 108.

1. Immediately after the bone marrow transplant, Andrea
   - ☐ a. lost most of her hair.
   - ☐ b. became nauseated.
   - ☐ c. showed no signs of improvement.
   - ☐ d. "pinked up."

2. The ravages of radiation treatment are
   - ☐ a. insignificant compared to the agony of chemotherapy.
   - ☐ b. more than most people can bear.
   - ☐ c. quickly overcome.
   - ☐ d. not immediately visible.

3. Andrea began her radiation treatments
   - ☐ a. before starting on chemotherapy.
   - ☐ b. after completing chemotherapy.
   - ☐ c. instead of chemotherapy.
   - ☐ d. while in the middle of chemotherapy.

4. Another title for this selection might be
   - ☐ a. "The Ends Do Not Justify the Means."
   - ☐ b. "The High Price of Healing."
   - ☐ c. "Is There a Doctor in the House?"
   - ☐ d. "The Miracle of Modern Technology."

5. Without a bone marrow transplant, victims of Hodgkin's disease would
   - ☐ a. experience minimal suffering.
   - ☐ b. recover quite slowly.
   - ☐ c. lose their hair.
   - ☐ d. die.

6. The author's attitude toward her patient is
   - ☐ a. unprofessional.
   - ☐ c. humane.
   - ☐ b. unjustified.
   - ☐ d. infuriating.

7. Treatment of Hodgkin's disease is
   - ☐ a. more painful than most medical procedures.
   - ☐ b. still experimental.
   - ☐ c. rarely attempted in people over the age of 30.
   - ☐ d. immensely rewarding for both the patient and the doctor.

8. The overall tone of the selection is
   - ☐ a. sorrowful.
   - ☐ c. sobering.
   - ☐ b. regretful.
   - ☐ d. sentimental.

9. When she saw Andrea suffering, the author felt
   - ☐ a. omnipotent.
   - ☐ c. disgusted.
   - ☐ b. helpless.
   - ☐ d. frightened.

10. The author's descriptions of medical procedures seem
    - ☐ a. imaginative.
    - ☐ c. realistic.
    - ☐ b. poetic.
    - ☐ d. exaggerated.

Comprehension Skills

1. recalling specific facts	6. making a judgment
2. retaining concepts	7. making an inference
3. organizing facts	8. recognizing tone
4. understanding the main idea	9. understanding characters
5. drawing a conclusion	10. appreciation of literary forms

Study Skills, Part One

Study Skills, Part One—Following is a passage with blanks where words have been omitted. Next to the passage are groups of five words, one group for each blank. Complete the passage by selecting the correct word for each of the blanks.

Good Listening, I

To help improve your listening habits, here are some positive steps you can take.

Prepare to Listen. Your attitude while attending class is important. If you feel that a particular class is a waste of time, you will obviously not be in the ___(1)___ to listen. It is difficult and almost impossible to get anything out of a lecture that you are not prepared for. To prepare, decide before class that the lecture period will be well spent; resolve to make it a ___(2)___ experience.

Another good way to prepare for a lecture is to keep ahead in your textbook and other required ___(3)___ . The more you know about a subject in advance, the more interested you will be in hearing what the instructor has to say about it. For prepared students, lectures become an ___(4)___ of ideas rather than a deluge of unfamiliar and seemingly unrelated facts.

Watch the Speaker. Don't take your eyes off of the speaker. When you look away, you invite ___(5)___ distractions that may compete for your attention. In class, you must listen with your eyes as well as with your ears.

Develop an awareness of the speaker's mannerisms. The gestures a speaker makes supplement his remarks. What a ___(6)___ does with punctuation, bold print, headlines, and italics, a speaker does with vocal inflection and body gestures. All speakers communicate ___(7)___ as well as orally. You must watch as you listen.

(1)			
	position		place
	mood	location	condition

(2)			
	depressing		frightening
	learning	helpful	recreational

(3)			
	writing		reading
	singing	playing	running

(4)			
	inspiration		exchange
	exclusion	expression	inspection

(5)			
	oral		intellectual
	visual	physical	muscular

(6)			
	actor		writer
	teacher	lawyer	student

(7)			
	physically		spiritually
	mentally	socially	successfully

Study Skills, Part Two—Read the study skills passage again, paying special attention to the lesson being taught. Then, without looking back at the passage, complete each sentence below by writing in the missing word or words. Check the Answer Key on page 108 for the answers to Study Skills, Part One, and Study Skills, Part Two.

1. It is important to attend class with a good _____ .

2. You will be more interested in the subject of the lecture if you read about it in _____ .

3. For unprepared students, lectures can be a series of unfamiliar and _____ facts.

4. In class, you must listen with your _____ as well as with your ears.

5. The speaker's _____ supplement his remarks.

20 | Women in Prison

by Sherrye Henry

Vocabulary—The five words below are from the story you are about to read. Study the words and their meanings. Then complete the ten sentences that follow, using one of the five words to fill in the blank in each sentence. Mark your answer by writing the letter of the word on the line before the sentence. Check your answers in the Answer Key on page 108.

A. harangued: lectured sternly; delivered a tirade

B. abundant: ample

C. incarcerated: put in jail

D. hideous: repulsive; despicable

E. recidivism: return to criminal activity

_____ 1. There is _____ evidence that women commit fewer violent crimes than men.

_____ 2. Some female ex-convicts have _____ their children about obeying the law.

_____ 3. Women who are _____ suffer by being separated from their children.

_____ 4. The rate of _____ is lower among women than among men.

_____ 5. Even women who are unwitting accomplices in drug deals are often _____ .

_____ 6. A small number of women are guilty of _____ crimes.

_____ 7. In prison, women have an _____ amount of time to contemplate their mistakes.

_____ 8. For years, officials have _____ the public about the dangers of drugs.

_____ 9. _____ might be reduced if convicts received job training.

_____ 10. Some gangs engage in the _____ torture of their victims.

Through the ages, poets have sung of the pain of misplaced affection, and mothers have harangued their daughters against getting mixed up with the wrong kind of man. Mama was right—especially in the case of a woman who breaks the law. Today, huge numbers of women are serving time in prisons because, at least in part, they ran around with the wrong guy.

Too many women fall for the line: "Baby, if you love me . . ." Then they go out and steal for their men.

Jackie Carroll is a daytime matron of Calcasieu Parish Jail in Lake Charles, La., whose inmates include women being held for trial, convicts serving time, and others awaiting transfer to state or federal prisons. She tells of women brought in with no idea why they are there: "One pregnant woman had been driving with her husband. She didn't know it, but the car was loaded with drugs. The cops pulled up, and here she is, charged with possession." Carroll explains the control men have over their women: "It's not that they say, 'Go steal this, go steal that.' Usually they'll say, 'Baby, if you love me . . .' and the woman will do anything for the man. The woman will ask him, 'You want a diamond? A watch?' They'll do their best to get it. And usually it's the man in a relationship who gets the drugs. He'll use his woman to set up the deal. Then, when an undercover narcotics agent slips in and buys, they're both busted."

Once exposed to the abundant and easy money that crime produces, many women willingly participate. Just released after serving seven years of a 10-year sentence, one tells of a man she called "The Godfather," who'd been stealing since he was 13 and taught her how to steal too:

"He took me all over the United States, traveling on other people's credit cards. Showed me how to hang paper [forge checks] and play the shots [pick pockets]. We were living good, didn't want for nothin'. Slept in the best hotels, as exclusive as you could find. I'd steal the credit cards in expensive restaurants. Just picked them up—people weren't paying attention. I was arrested 13 times. Each time, they let me out on bail because I used an alias and had no record. Then we'd move on. We were finally identified in Washington when my guy ran a red light in a rented car. Yes, I *liked* him, but he frightened me. Some nights he sent me out to steal on my own, which I don't like to do—I always like someone to protect my back. And when I got cracked, he'd leave me in jail overnight, let me lay up there, worrying about how I'm going to get back home. It's the guys, all right. They're no good for you. But I *liked* him."

Another former prisoner, though just 25, has had enough bad experiences with men for several lifetimes. "When I was 16," she says, "I ran into this guy and had my son by him. He used to sell a lot of drugs and began beating up on me, smoking 'dust,' bugging out. I left him when

I was 21, but I had learned a lot. All the stuff I had seen him doing, I started doing—buying my own drugs, selling. Then, at 22, I met this other guy who had got beat up by some big dope fiend, so I gave him some work, selling. He began coming around, bringing his big cocaine. I never dealt in cocaine, but I was getting greedy—wanting the extra money. One day, he asked if I'd go out of the country and bring some in. I was almost out of the airport door when the police snatched me. They had got him first and evidently he told on me—because we weren't together—although he still denies it."

Karl Rasmussen, executive director of the Women's Prison Association in New York, says he hears similar stories often. "It's tragic," he says, "but no surprise that men use women for their own purposes—they've been doing that for centuries, for sex or greed. Men aren't driven to crime by a relationship the way women are. It may sound sexist, but men are apt to have higher expectations for themselves. In our mixed society of races and cultures, what we all have in common is understanding the value of the dollar, and the drive to be materially successful seems to affect men more than it does women."

But the effort to survive in our increasingly materialistic society is what ultimately sends most women offenders to prison. Largely lacking in skills, self-esteem, and the experience of knowing women in their own lives who can function well and independently as wage-earners, they react to life ultimately by resorting to crime. Essentially, they want; they see; they take. Charlotte Nesbitt, program manager at the American Correctional Association in College Park, Md., cites a nationwide study done by the association in 1983. She notes that the report profiles the average female prison population this way: "54 percent are white, 46 percent are non-white. Most (75 percent) are between the ages of 25 and 34, single, mothers, and unemployed at the time they committed the crime; 51 percent are serving time for a crime against property." Says Nesbitt, "They simply weren't coping, so the women did something to survive by their standards."

Jackie Carroll agrees. "Nobody likes to be poor," she says. "Mostly, they sell the stuff they steal. That's how they pay the light bill or get money for milk or clothes. That's how they survive."

Historically, the low-skilled illiterates in our society, involved with an intoxicating substance, have filled our prisons. "That hasn't changed," says Rasmussen. "A hundred and fifty years ago, it was poor whites—their names were often Irish—and alcohol abuse. Today, it's poor minorities and drug abuse." He says he's convinced that higher socioeconomic groups commit the same amount of crime, but they aren't caught as often and are better able to beat the charges when they are caught, often because they can hire better attorneys. It has always been true, if not just, that those who end up in prison are less educated, poorer, and have fewer family resources.

Drugs have shattered our culture in many ways. "Although only 9 percent of female convictions are specifically for substance abuse," says Charlotte Nesbitt, "crimes against persons and against property frequently involve drugs in some fashion." And this is not always because of addiction but often because of the profit motive. "Years ago," says Karl Rasmussen, "we thought addicts sold drugs to support their habits. Now we also have unaddicted, uneducated women who can make thousands of dollars a day just by selling drugs."

If men often lead women to crime through love or threats or by abandoning them and their children, there is one point at which men and women criminals generally part company: at the point of a gun.

Jackie Carroll of Calcasieu Parish Jail says women seldom use guns. "They may be involved—they may be sitting in a car—but a woman going in with a shotgun or a handgun? I haven't seen it here. Maybe it's because of the way they're raised here. Maybe the big cities are different."

I asked some women about the use of violence. "It's not necessary," says the former prisoner who once stole credit cards nationwide. "Selling drugs—that's hurting people. Stealing—isn't that enough damage right there? We women have more finesse than men. Men don't care—they'll hurt you."

There are a few exceptions: 10 percent of women convicts were incarcerated for violent crimes, including women who abused their children and battered women who attacked their partners. This percentage hasn't changed in more than 20 years. But the vast majority of women in prison are there for what some call the "gentler" crimes of larceny, theft, embezzlement, forgery, and fraud. And even these crimes are committed mostly by amateurs.

"Crime isn't of great interest to most women," says Rasmussen. "It's generally something they get caught up in, circumstantially, as they get caught up with a guy. Women don't make a practice of crime. And there's a cruelty you see in men more than in women—a primitive thing. When women kill, they kill out of frustration, not knowing how else to deal with the situation. With women, you rarely see cases of torture, then killing. It's there, sometimes, with child abuse, but every woman child-abuser I've seen was abused herself as a child."

But when women *are* violent, the stories often are hideous. A group of former offenders shook their heads in disgust at recalling a woman involved with a motorcycle gang whose members had murdered several people. "They nailed a guy to the floor through his knees," said one. "She had to do it too—to maintain her position in the group."

Vicious, hardened female criminals are rare, however. The vast majority go to jail once and choose never to return, for they are terribly punished—not so much by the incarceration, or by being deprived of the man they loved, but by being separated from their children.

Certainly, their guilt and pain is obvious when women discuss how their imprisonment affects their children. A Louisiana check-forger recounts with embarrassment how one of her children came home and asked her to verify a neighbor's report that she'd been seen making bail at court: " 'Mama,' my child asked, 'don't you know how it makes us feel when they say that?' I said 'yeah.' And I do—we all honestly do. A piece of us dies when they say that. I've watched my daughters suffer. Not from the loss of love—they've got that by tons—but from the missing person they depended on. Me. Still, the kids don't stop loving you, and you don't quit trying to teach them the right way."

Recidivism among prisoners is higher for men than for women. Perhaps this is because, as many of the women told me, they gained something positive from the experience. "I'm not glad I got arrested," says the drug dealer who was caught at an airport, "but it may be a blessing. I could be anywhere now. When I got involved with those cocaine dealers, they could have had me take that trip for them and then killed me when I got back." A prisoner who was a heavy user and dealer of drugs for 20 years says, "At first I was annoyed at the judge who sentenced me, for interfering with my life. I was surviving. But I was miserable, dopesick, always depressed. I started drinking. When I went to prison, I cleaned up completely, so it was a bad experience with good results."

Coming out of prison is often as frightening as going in. Generally, the women have no more education or job skills than they had before imprisonment, and no fewer family responsibilities. "I don't know what's ahead," says the former credit-card-stealing, first-class traveler. "I hope I can find me some work to make some use of myself. My kids are okay. My mother has been raising them just fine. But I don't know about me. I'm not lying: I'm tired of jail, I'm getting too old for that. It ain't no life. God knows, it ain't no life. But I *don't* know about me."

A sign on the warden's door in the Calcasieu Parish Jail reads: "We don't promise you a rose garden." Inside the jail, one gaunt, toothless prisoner of indeterminate age contemplates her past and her future: "I don't have a husband," she says, "I forged checks to buy things for my kids for Christmas. Just took a lady's checkbook and started cashing checks and got two-and-a-half years. I've been here a number of times—90 days for food-stamp fraud, 60 days for shoplifting. I have three kids in foster care, three grown. When I get out, I hope I don't do it again—but I don't know, I just don't know."

Starting Time		Finishing Time	
Reading Time		Reading Rate	
Comprehension		Vocabulary	

Comprehension— Read the following questions and statements. For each one, put an *x* in the box before the option that contains the most complete or accurate answer. Check your answers in the Answer Key on page 108.

1. Usually women who are child-abusers
   - ☐ a. are intimidated by men.
   - ☐ b. have a history of drug abuse.
   - ☐ c. were themselves abused as children.
   - ☐ d. come from the lowest socioeconomic class.

2. Many women become caught up in crime in order to
   - ☐ a. experience a thrill.
   - ☐ b. get money.
   - ☐ c. punish their families.
   - ☐ d. impress their children.

3. One hundred and fifty years ago, most female prisoners were
   - ☐ a. unmarried.
   - ☐ b. immigrants.
   - ☐ c. alcoholics.
   - ☐ d. insane.

4. Many women are
   - ☐ a. unable to handle long-term relationships.
   - ☐ b. inherently violent.
   - ☐ c. born criminals.
   - ☐ d. led astray by men.

5. When women are released from prison, they often have
   - ☐ a. no way of earning a living.
   - ☐ b. an uncontrollable drug problem.
   - ☐ c. a built-in support system.
   - ☐ d. a grudge against society.

6. It is important for women in prison to
   - ☐ a. forget about their past lives.
   - ☐ b. rely on guards for protection.
   - ☐ c. develop friendships with other prisoners.
   - ☐ d. maintain contact with their children.

7. Men are more likely than women to
   - ☐ a. abuse their children.
   - ☐ b. blame society for their problems.
   - ☐ c. use a gun.
   - ☐ d. express remorse for their crimes.

8. The tone of the final paragraph is
   - ☐ a. uplifting.
   - ☐ b. bleak.
   - ☐ c. humorous.
   - ☐ d. angry.

9. Men who entice women to commit crimes are
   - ☐ a. insecure.
   - ☐ b. intelligent.
   - ☐ c. introspective.
   - ☐ d. opportunistic.

10. The statement that "now we also have unaddicted, uneducated women who can make thousands of dollars a day just by selling drugs" is an example of
    - ☐ a. overstatement.
    - ☐ b. a metaphor.
    - ☐ c. literal language.
    - ☐ d. figurative language.

Comprehension Skills

1. recalling specific facts	6. making a judgment
2. retaining concepts	7. making an inference
3. organizing facts	8. recognizing tone
4. understanding the main idea	9. understanding characters
5. drawing a conclusion	10. appreciation of literary forms

Study Skills, Part One—Following is a passage with blanks where words have been omitted. Next to the passage are groups of five words, one group for each blank. Complete the passage by selecting the correct word for each of the blanks.

Good Listening, II

Note Questions. Listen closely to questions asked in class. When an instructor asks a question, he or she is probably about to ___(1)___ something important and is calling for your attention. This is an important signal between a speaker and the listeners.

Speakers' questions are designed to help you listen and

(1)   discuss   dismiss
       approach   retract   omit

learn. You should also notice questions asked by others in the class. Student questions signal the instructor; they indicate how the (2) is coming across. The instructor will elaborate and illustrate, repeat and paraphrase, to help the listeners understand the matter. Questions from both teacher and (3) are valuable; pay attention to them.

Listen Creatively. You should not think about other things while listening to a speaker; you must give your (4) attention to the speaker's words.

Ask Questions. If questions are not (5) during a class session, write your questions in your notebook and get the answers later.

Bring Questions to Class. Your attention is sharpened when you are listening for answers. If your instructor calls for class participation don't be afraid or shy about speaking up. Your attention is (6) most sharply when you are on the firing line; and if you are mistaken and you are corrected in class, you won't be likely to forget the correct response at exam time.

Your success in school will depend largely on how well you listen in class. If applied, the suggestions offered here can substantially improve your ability in this (7) area.

(2)	appearance		voice
	intention	enthusiasm	message

(3)	principal		employer
	student	friend	parent

(4)	polite		partial
	superficial	entire	apparent

(5)	probable		rejected
	announced	permitted	programmed

(6)	attracted		denied
	focused	damaged	forgotten

(7)	unimportant		vital
	attractive	neutral	controversial

Study Skills, Part Two—Read the study skills passage again, paying special attention to the lesson being taught. Then, without looking back at the passage, complete each sentence below by writing in the missing word or words. Check the Answer Key on page 108 for the answers to Study Skills, Part One, and Study Skills, Part Two.

1. Instructors use questions as a way to call for _____ .

2. The instructor's question is an important _____ between an instructor and the listeners.

3. When you listen, do not _____ about other things.

4. Your attention is sharpened when you are _____ for answers.

5. If you are mistaken and corrected in class, you will not _____ the correct response later.

Answer Key

Selection 1

Vocabulary

1. B	6. B
2. C	7. E
3. E	8. A
4. A	9. D
5. D	10. C

Comprehension

1. b	6. b
2. a	7. b
3. d	8. a
4. c	9. c
5. c	10. d

Study Skills, Part One

1. effectiveness	6. lure
2. introductory	7. devices
3. anecdote	
4. concepts	
5. significance	

Study Skills, Part Two

1. paragraphs
2. printed page
3. announcement
4. previewing
5. words

Selection 2

Vocabulary

1. C	6. C
2. D	7. E
3. E	8. D
4. A	9. A
5. B	10. B

Comprehension

1. b	6. a
2. c	7. b
3. a	8. a
4. a	9. a
5. d	10. d

Study Skills, Part One

1. understand	6. flexible
2. similar	7. linger
3. composed	
4. limitations	
5. clarify	

Study Skills, Part Two

1. idea
2. students
3. misunderstood
4. speed
5. new

Selection 3

Vocabulary

1. B	6. A
2. C	7. D
3. E	8. A
4. D	9. E
5. B	10. C

Comprehension

1. d	6. c
2. b	7. a
3. d	8. c
4. a	9. c
5. a	10. b

Study Skills, Part One

1. subject	6. Expect
2. facts	7. present
3. examined	
4. introduce	
5. logically	

Study Skills, Part Two

1. facts
2. instructional
3. reasons
4. learning
5. study

Selection 4

Vocabulary

1. A	6. B
2. E	7. D
3. A	8. B
4. E	9. C
5. D	10. C

Comprehension

1. c	6. a
2. c	7. b
3. b	8. a
4. a	9. d
5. c	10. d

Study Skills, Part One

1. topic	6. comprehension
2. new	7. Consequently
3. essential	
4. precisely	
5. definition	

Study Skills, Part Two

1. recognizable
2. italics
3. key
4. information
5. contribution

Selection 5

Vocabulary

1. C	6. A
2. B	7. E
3. D	8. E
4. B	9. D
5. C	10. A

Comprehension

1. b	6. c
2. a	7. c
3. c	8. a
4. b	9. b
5. b	10. a

Study Skills, Part One

1. implies	6. contribution
2. change	7. roles
3. preview	
4. arouse	
5. summing	

Study Skills, Part Two

1. short
2. ending
3. introduction
4. concluding
5. functions

Selection 6

Vocabulary

1. C	6. A
2. A	7. D
3. E	8. E
4. C	9. B
5. B	10. D

Comprehension

1. d	6. b
2. d	7. b
3. b	8. b
4. c	9. a
5. b	10. b

Study Skills, Part One

1. recognizing	6. developed
2. obvious	7. techniques
3. final	
4. important	
5. summarize	

Study Skills, Part Two

1. conclusion
2. facts
3. reviewing
4. speaker
5. moral

Selection 7

Vocabulary

1. E	6. B
2. C	7. D
3. D	8. C
4. A	9. B
5. E	10. A

Comprehension

1. c	6. c
2. b	7. a
3. d	8. b
4. d	9. c
5. b	10. b

Study Skills, Part One

1. described	6. progress
2. studying	7. habits
3. mastery	
4. plods	
5. aloud	

Study Skills, Part Two

1. inflexible
2. 100 percent
3. specialized
4. taught
5. conditioned

Selection 8

Vocabulary

1. D	6. C
2. A	7. E
3. B	8. C
4. E	9. D
5. A	10. B

Comprehension

1. d	6. a
2. a	7. c
3. c	8. c
4. a	9. b
5. c	10. c

Study Skills, Part One

1. skilled	6. comprehended
2. analytical	7. appropriate
3. skimming	
4. casual	
5. nonproductive	

Study Skills, Part Two

1. varies
2. slow
3. rapid
4. concepts
5. skimming

Selection 9

Vocabulary

1. B	6. C
2. D	7. D
3. E	8. A
4. C	9. B
5. A	10. E

Comprehension

1. b	6. a
2. c	7. d
3. b	8. c
4. d	9. a
5. b	10. a

Study Skills, Part One

1. specific	6. Paragraphs
2. employed	7. skipped
3. information	
4. graphic	
5. factual	

Study Skills, Part Two

1. careless
2. study-type
3. title
4. definitions
5. reference

Selection 10

Vocabulary

1. E	6. A
2. C	7. D
3. A	8. C
4. B	9. B
5. D	10. E

Comprehension

1. a	6. a
2. b	7. a
3. b	8. c
4. c	9. d
5. c	10. a

Study Skills, Part One

1. impressive	6. difficult
2. value	7. fill
3. necessary	
4. perform	
5. trigger	

Study Skills, Part Two

1. dynamic
2. Previewing
3. ideas
4. Rereading
5. easy

Selection 11

Vocabulary

1. A	6. B
2. E	7. E
3. D	8. D
4. C	9. C
5. A	10. B

Comprehension

1. d	6. b
2. c	7. d
3. c	8. d
4. b	9. d
5. a	10. a

Study Skills, Part One

1. specialized	6. new
2. reward	7. foundation
3. appropriate	
4. teacher	
5. learning	

Study Skills, Part Two

1. mastered
2. understanding
3. knowledge
4. background
5. uninteresting

Selection 12

Vocabulary

1. E	6. A
2. C	7. D
3. E	8. B
4. D	9. A
5. B	10. C

Comprehension

1. b	6. a
2. d	7. d
3. b	8. a
4. d	9. c
5. b	10. a

Study Skills, Part One

1. emphasizes	6. exact
2. points	7. specialized
3. stress	
4. quizzing	
5. more	

Study Skills, Part Two

1. instructors
2. identify
3. repeated
4. questions
5. precise

Selection 13

Vocabulary

1. E	6. D
2. A	7. B
3. B	8. A
4. D	9. E
5. C	10. C

Comprehension

1. b	6. c
2. c	7. d
3. c	8. a
4. d	9. c
5. b	10. c

Study Skills, Part One

1. chapter	6. enrich
2. headings	7. bonus
3. located	
4. following	
5. class	

Study Skills, Part Two

1. major
2. summaries
3. definitions
4. increase
5. interest

Selection 14

Vocabulary

1. D	6. B
2. C	7. A
3. E	8. A
4. D	9. C
5. E	10. B

Comprehension

1. b	6. c
2. d	7. c
3. d	8. c
4. c	9. d
5. b	10. a

Study Skills, Part One

1. need	6. demonstrating
2. sorted	7. vocabulary
3. notes	
4. review	
5. before	

Study Skills, Part Two

1. alphabetically
2. notebook
3. studied
4. memory
5. Precise

Selection 15

Vocabulary

1. E	6. E
2. B	7. B
3. A	8. A
4. C	9. D
5. D	10. C

Comprehension

1. a	6. b
2. a	7. a
3. c	8. a
4. c	9. a
5. c	10. a

Study Skills, Part One

1. reading	6. permanent
2. writing	7. word
3. familiar	
4. list	
5. confusion	

Study Skills, Part Two

1. better
2. speaking
3. shades
4. used
5. added

Selection 16

Vocabulary

1. D	6. E
2. A	7. C
3. B	8. A
4. B	9. D
5. C	10. E

Comprehension

1. c	6. a
2. a	7. c
3. a	8. c
4. b	9. d
5. c	10. b

Study Skills, Part One

1. meaning	6. difficult
2. adjective	7. evaluated
3. stems	
4. acquired	
5. explained	

Study Skills, Part Two

1. beginning
2. end
3. based
4. dictionary
5. educated

Selection 17

Vocabulary

1. B	6. D
2. A	7. A
3. E	8. E
4. C	9. C
5. B	10. D

Comprehension

1. a	6. d
2. a	7. d
3. d	8. c
4. c	9. b
5. c	10. d

Study Skills, Part One

1. correct	5. association
2. misunder-	6. recollection
standing	7. think
3. another	
4. directions	

Study Skills, Part Two

1. faulty
2. industry
3. credit
4. everyone
5. daydream

Selection 18

Vocabulary

1. D	6. C
2. E	7. A
3. B	8. E
4. A	9. C
5. D	10. B

Comprehension

1. b	6. a
2. c	7. a
3. c	8. a
4. d	9. d
5. b	10. c

Study Skills, Part One

1. contrary	6. Attack
2. interferes	7. judged
3. pretend	
4. impression	
5. hard	

Study Skills, Part Two

1. Closed-mindedness
2. attention
3. discuss
4. futility
5. content

Selection 19

Vocabulary

1. C	6. A
2. D	7. C
3. E	8. D
4. E	9. A
5. B	10. B

Comprehension

1. c	6. c
2. d	7. a
3. a	8. c
4. b	9. b
5. d	10. c

Study Skills, Part One

1. mood	6. writer
2. learning	7. physically
3. reading	
4. exchange	
5. visual	

Study Skills, Part Two

1. attitude
2. advance
3. unrelated
4. eyes
5. gestures

Selection 20

Vocabulary

1. B	6. D
2. A	7. B
3. C	8. A
4. E	9. E
5. C	10. D

Comprehension

1. c	6. d
2. b	7. c
3. c	8. b
4. d	9. d
5. a	10. c

Study Skills, Part One

1. discuss	6. focused
2. message	7. vital
3. student	
4. entire	
5. permitted	

Study Skills, Part Two

1. attention
2. signal
3. think
4. listening
5. forget

Bibliography

Every effort has been made to locate the author, publisher, place of publication, and copyright date for each selection.

Angelou, Maya. "Letter from France" from "Berkeley to James Baldwin and Back." In *Holiday* magazine. Holiday Magazine, 1974.

Asimov, Isaac. "Lost in Space." In *Discover* magazine. New York: Nightfall, Inc., 1988.

Bradbury, Ray. "The Pedestrian." In *The Golden Apples of the Sun*. Harold Matson Company, Inc., 1953.

Friedan, Betty. *The Feminine Mystique*. New York: W.W. Norton & Company, Inc., 1963.

Goldstone, Herbert. "Virtuoso." In *The Magazine of Fantasy and Science Fiction*. Connecticut: Mercury Press, Inc., 1952.

Helminiak, Ray. "First Flight Across America." In *Northliner*. North Central Airlines.

Henry, Sherrye. "Women in Prison." In *Parade* magazine. New York: Parade Publications, 1988.

Joey, with Dave Fisher. *Killer: Autobiography of a Mafia Hit Man*. Chicago: The Playboy Press, 1973.

McGough, Elizabeth. "Body Language Spoken Here." In *American Youth* magazine. American Youth Magazine, 1972.

Palcewski, John. "Curbing Cab Crime in Chicago." In *Olin* magazine. Olin Corporation.

Parker, Dorothy. "The Standard of Living." In *The Portable Dorothy Parker*. New York: The Viking Press, 1941.

Phillips, McCandlish. "Aged Wait in Stony Silence, but Not for Buses." In *The New York Times*. New York: The New York Times Company, 1970.

Reno, June Mellies. "The Day I Nearly Drowned." In *Good Housekeeping* magazine. New York: Hearst Corporation, 1974.

Rosenthal, Elisabeth. "When Pain Is the Only Choice." In *Discover* magazine. New York: Family Media, 1988.

Ross, Irwin. "Henry Ford's Fabulous Flivver." In *Our Sun*. Sun Oil Company.

Rosten, Norman. *Marilyn: An Untold Story*. New York: New American Library, 1973.

Saki [H.H. Munro]. "The Open Window." In *The Complete Short Stories of Saki*. New York: The Viking Press.

Scott, Willard. "Golden Oldies." In *America, My Back Yard*. New York: Simon & Schuster, Inc., 1987.

Stone, Judith. "Velcro: The Final Frontier." In *Discover* magazine. New York: Family Media, 1988.

Words per Minute

Selection / No. of Words	20	19	18	17	16	15	14	13	12	11	10	9	8	7	6	5	4	3	2	1
No. of Words	1980	1990	1980	1680	1215	1785	1750	1795	2020	1265	2010	1810	1530	1455	1685	1300	1795	1435	2020	1585
1:20	1520	1540	1520	1295	915	1340	1325	1350	1520	950	1510	1360	1150	1095	1265	985	1350	1080	1520	1220
1:40	1235	1250	1235	1010	730	1075	1060	1080	1215	760	1210	1090	920	875	1015	790	1080	865	1215	990
2:00	985	1000	985	840	610	895	880	900	1010	635	1005	905	765	730	845	655	900	720	1010	790
2:20	860	870	860	720	520	765	775	770	865	545	865	775	655	625	735	560	770	615	865	690
2:40	760	770	760	630	455	670	660	675	760	475	755	680	575	545	635	490	675	540	760	610
3:00	660	665	660	560	405	595	585	600	675	420	670	605	525	485	560	435	600	480	675	560
3:20	600	605	600	505	365	535	530	540	605	380	605	545	460	435	505	395	540	430	605	510
3:40	550	555	550	460	330	490	480	490	550	345	550	495	420	400	460	360	490	395	550	440
4:00	495	500	495	420	305	445	440	450	505	315	505	455	385	365	420	330	450	360	505	395
4:20	460	465	460	390	280	410	405	415	465	290	465	420	355	335	390	305	415	330	465	370
4:40	430	435	430	360	260	385	380	385	435	270	430	390	330	310	360	280	385	310	435	345
5:00	395	400	395	335	245	355	350	360	405	255	400	360	305	290	335	260	360	290	405	315
5:20	370	375	370	315	230	335	330	335	380	235	375	340	285	275	315	245	335	270	380	300
5:40	350	355	350	295	215	315	310	315	355	225	355	320	270	255	300	230	315	255	355	285
6:00	330	335	330	280	205	300	295	300	335	210	335	300	255	245	280	220	300	240	335	265
6:20	315	315	315	265	190	280	280	285	320	200	320	285	240	230	265	205	285	225	320	250
6:40	300	305	300	250	180	270	265	270	305	190	300	270	230	220	255	195	270	215	305	240
7:00	280	285	280	240	175	255	250	255	290	180	285	260	220	210	240	185	255	205	290	225
7:20	270	275	270	230	165	245	240	245	275	175	275	245	210	200	230	180	245	195	275	215
7:40	260	265	260	220	160	235	230	235	265	165	260	235	200	190	220	170	235	195	265	210
8:00	245	250	245	210	150	225	220	225	255	160	250	225	190	180	210	165	225	180	255	200
8:20	240	240	240	200	145	215	210	215	240	150	240	215	185	175	205	155	215	170	240	190
8:40	230	230	230	195	140	205	205	205	235	145	230	210	175	170	195	150	205	165	235	185
9:00	220	220	220	185	135	200	195	200	225	140	225	200	170	160	185	145	200	160	225	175
9:20	210	215	210	180	130	190	190	190	215	135	215	195	165	155	180	140	190	155	215	170
9:40	205	210	205	175	125	185	180	185	210	130	210	185	160	150	175	135	185	150	210	165
10:00	195	200	195	170	120	180	175	180	200	125	200	180	155	145	170	130	180	145	200	160
10:20	190	195	190	165	120	175	170	175	195	120	195	175	150	140	165	125	175	140	195	155
10:40	185	190	185	160	115	170	165	170	190	120	190	170	145	135	160	125	170	135	190	150
11:00	180	180	180	155	110	160	160	165	185	115	185	165	140	130	155	120	165	130	185	145
11:20	175	175	175	150	105	160	155	160	180	110	175	160	135	130	150	115	160	125	180	140
11:40	170	170	170	145	105	155	150	155	175	110	170	155	130	125	145	110	155	125	175	135
12:00	165	165	165	140	100	150	145	150	170	105	170	150	130	120	140	110	150	120	170	130
12:20	160	160	160	135	100	145	145	145	165	100	165	145	125	120	135	105	145	115	165	130
12:40	155	160	155	135	95	140	140	140	160	100	160	140	120	115	135	105	140	115	160	125
13:00	150	155	150	130	95	140	135	140	155	95	155	140	120	110	130	100	140	110	155	120
13:20	150	150	150	125	90	135	130	135	150	95	150	135	115	110	125	100	135	110	150	120
13:40	145	145	145	125	90	130	130	130	150	90	145	135	110	105	125	95	130	105	150	115
14:00	140	140	140	120	85	130	125	130	145	90	145	130	110	105	120	95	130	105	145	115
14:20	140	140	140	120	85	125	125	125	140	85	140	125	105	100	120	90	125	100	140	110
14:40	135	135	135	115	85	120	120	120	140	85	135	125	105	100	115	90	120	100	140	110
15:00	130	135	130	110	80	120	120	120	135		135	120	100	95	110	85	120	95	135	105

Minutes and Seconds Elapsed

Progress Graph

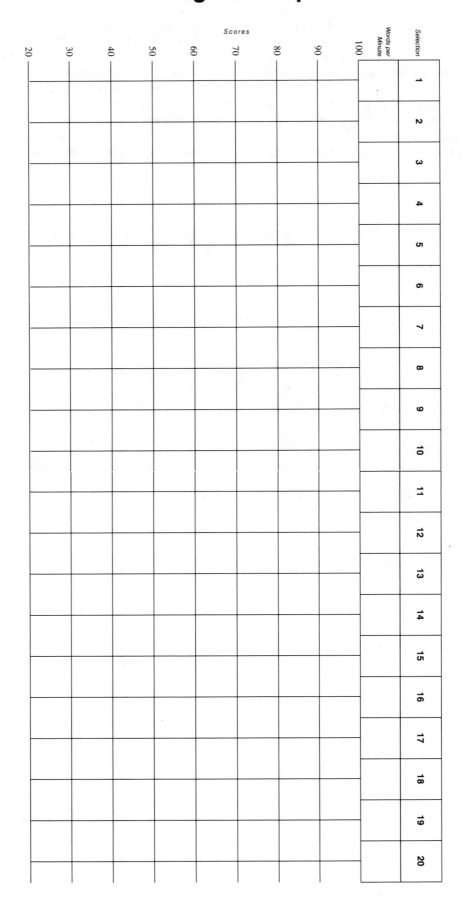

Comprehension Skills Profile

The graph below is designed to help you see your areas of comprehension weakness. Because all the comprehension questions in this text are coded, it is possible for you to determine which kinds of questions give you the most trouble.

On the graph below, keep a record of questions you have answered incorrectly. Following each selection, darken a square on the graph next to the number of the question missed. The columns are labeled with the selection numbers.

By looking at the chart and noting the number of shaded squares, you should be able to tell which areas of comprehension you are weak in. A large number of shaded squares across from a particular skill signifies an area of reading comprehension weakness. When you discover a particular weakness, give greater attention and time to answering questions of that type.

Further, you might wish to check with your instructor for recommendations of appropriate practice materials.

Selection

Categories of Comprehension Skills	1	2	3	4	5	6	7	8	9	10	11	12	13	14	15	16	17	18	19	20
1. Recalling Specific Facts																				
2. Retaining Concepts																				
3. Organizing Facts																				
4. Understanding the Main Idea																				
5. Drawing a Conclusion																				
6. Making a Judgment																				
7. Making an Inference																				
8. Recognizing Tone																				
9. Understanding Characters																				
10. Appreciation of Literary Forms																				